מעיני הישועה

ספר שמות

A Livable Truth

Inspiring Reflections on the Book of Exodus

Rabbi Shu Eliovson

Infinite thanks to HaShem, my Eishet Chayil Hila,
my Parents, my Children, my Siblings, my Chevreh,
& All Who Have Touched my Journey Along the Way

Printed in the United States of America

First Printing, 2024

ISBN: 978-1-7360642-2-1

Good Judaism Publishing
235 Etrog Street
Moshav Shuva 8514700
Israel

www.SamuraiStory.com
shu@SamuraiStory.com

Table of Contents

Week 13: The Torah Portion of 'Shemot'

Remember Who You Are

It's hard to understand what that Burning Bush is all about. Without a doubt, it demonstrated some pretty cool special effects. And even Moses (Moshe Rabbeinu) was like, "I gotta check this out. It's so, so strange!"

But why? There are a lot of ways that we can imagine God appearing to someone. For instance, the whole Mount Sinai thing — that seems more along the power-vibe of God. And the Ten Plagues are a pretty awesome show-of-force! The Splitting the Sea was incredible, too!

But the Burning Bush? What is that about, exactly? Why was that the opening show, so to speak? Why was the Burning Bush the first impression that God wanted to make on Moshe? Why was it the first symbol to be used in the birth of the Jewish Nation?

Let's go a little bit further, just in case things aren't confusing enough. Moshe says to God, "I understand that you want me to go to Egypt, and act as an agent on Your behalf. But why would anyone believe me? Why would anyone believe in a single individual, standing up against the empire of Egypt?! *"Hey, God sent me. I'm going to liberate you from brutal and serious bondage. No, I don't have a nuclear arsenal at my disposal. I'm not coming in with an entire cavalry, with horses and soldiers. Just me. I'm gonna do it."* Yeah, right…

And so God says, "Oh! Good question. Alright. I'm going to give you some signs! And when you do these signs, well, everyone will know it's the real deal!"

OK, so these have to be some pretty impressive signs, right?

So God says, "What do you have in your hand there, Moshe?"

And Moshe says, "Well, I have this walking stick…"

And God says, "Nice. Alright, throw it down on the ground."

Moshe throws it down.

It turns into a snake!

"Oh my goodness!" Moshe freaks out. He steps back.

And we can understand why Moshe would freak out. Because if any of us had a walking stick that was six feet long, and all of a sudden it turned into a big snake — yeah, that would definitely alarm us!

But it's not really clear how that would convince an entire nation living in bondage and having their children murdered, to suddenly say, "Oh! This guy who turns sticks into snakes, obviously he's here to set us free!" Especially since in next week's Torah portion we see that Pharaoh's magicians were able to do the same thing!

Then God tells him, "Now, grab that snake by its tail." So, Moshe does. He overcomes his fear, grabs it by the tail, and Poof! — it's a staff again.

Nice. Neat trick. Cool trick, definitely. But how is this a sign of imminent liberation?

So God says, "OK, I've got another sign for you! Check this out! Stick your hand inside your tunic." So Moshe slides his hand in. "OK, take it out!", God says. Moshe takes it out.

Poof! Whoah!! His entire hand is leprous! That's kind of crazy. And God says, "Stick it back in again." Moshe does it. "Pull it out", says God. And his hand is normal again.

Clearly the sign of a great Liberator of Nations, right? With that kind of a hat-trick, there's *no way* that Pharaoh could get in Moshe's way, right? Hmmm…

And then God says, "Alright, if that's not enough, I've got one more crazy trick! When you get there, if those first two don't work, take a cup and scoop some water out of the Nile river and throw it on the ground and that water will turn into blood!!"

Moshe is like, "Alright, I'm good with this!"

Now, if Moshe was good with this, obviously he understood something, and it made sense to him. But what was it? Because these signs ultimately don't work out very well. No-one jumped to attention in Egypt when Moshe performed these 'magical acts'. Yet Moshe still felt good about them.

What is the significance of the Burning Bush? What were the deeper meanings of the signs that God provided to Moshe, that put Moshe at ease? What was the deeper meaning of the initial conversation between Moshe and HaShem? And what was the comforting answer that HaShem explained to Moshe, which finally gave Moshe the confidence to return to Egypt and to confront Pharaoh?

We'll come back to these questions and their illuminating answers a bit later. But first…

Consider the way things played out: Moshe and Aharon go before Pharaoh and they tell him, "You gotta do this. You gotta let these people go. They want to go serve their God. And God wants them to come serve Him. If you don't let them go, it's going to get really bad…"

But Pharaoh refuses. And not only does he refuse, but he decides to double down on the labor of the Jewish nation. He stops providing them with the straw that they need to make their bricks, yet makes them keep the same work production levels, despite the added task of harvesting the straw for themselves! Now they're not even being given the raw materials!

But look what happens, because this is important: The people come to Moshe and Aharon and they say, "You've put the sword in Pharaoh's hand to make our lives more horrible than they have been until now. You gave him the ammunition to accuse us of being lazy!! As if things weren't bad enough…"

But there is a strange thing here, in the anger of the people. The Children of Israel seem to be drawing a separation between what is happening to them, and the agents that are causing it. They *do not* question God or lose faith in Him over their increased misfortune - in fact they invoke God's justice as a judgement against Moshe and Aharon!

וַיֹּאמְרוּ אֲלֵהֶם יֵרֶא ה' עֲלֵיכֶם וְיִשְׁפֹּט אֲשֶׁר הִבְאַשְׁתֶּם אֶת־רֵיחֵנוּ בְּעֵינֵי
פַרְעֹה וּבְעֵינֵי עֲבָדָיו לָתֶת־חֶרֶב בְּיָדָם לְהָרְגֵנוּ

"The fear of God should be upon the two of you. For God will judge your behavior, that you made us look bad in the eyes of Pharaoh and his servants, and you've put a sword in their hands to afflict us yet even more." (5:21)

What powerful words. They don't question God. They'll deal with their 'fate' on their own. But they have a message for these agents that have played a role in the mess they now find themselves in! They say to Moshe and Aharon: "You need to face God regarding what you've done! You should have an awe, a fear of God, who will judge you for this, because you did something wrong."

And Moshe and Aharon, they go before God and they say, "They're right! How can this be?"

And God says, "Well, I was actually looking for that prayer! I was looking for them to manifest such a deep core of Faith. Because it's that realization, that clarity of Faith, which will ultimately transform their destiny and bring redemption."

It's interesting what God says when he talks about seeing the plight of the Jewish people. God says to Moshe:

וְעַתָּה הִנֵּה צַעֲקַת בְּנֵי־יִשְׂרָאֵל בָּאָה אֵלָי

"Behold, the cry of the Children of Israel has come to me..."

וְגַם־רָאִיתִי אֶת־הַלַּחַץ אֲשֶׁר מִצְרַיִם לֹחֲצִים אֹתָם

*"…and I have **also seen** the pressure, the brutality through which Egypt is oppressing them." (Shemot 3:9)*

Interesting separation.
Aren't they one and the same?

This is an important observation and question, because it lends towards another, connected question: Why were Pharaoh and Egypt punished for what they did to the Jewish people? After all, in the Book of Genesis when God makes his covenant with Abraham, he tells him about this bondage and what will happen to his descendants. So weren't Pharaoh and the Egyptian people simply fulfilling God's word?

And the answer is something very, very deep. The answer is: While it may have been the destiny of the Children of Israel to endure this bondage, *it didn't have to be Pharaoh and the Egyptians who put them through it.*

It's a profound idea.

It means that if I get punched in the face by somebody, *two separate events* have actually taken place:
1) The person who punched me in the face has an issue with their behavior and their act of violence, and what it means in terms of their character.
2) The fact that I got punched in the face is actually *a conversation going on between me and my Divine life-story*. It means it is an integral part of my journey in this lifetime *to get punched in the face today*, and if it hadn't been that person, it would have been another person.

To be clear, we are not talking about fatalism. 'Destiny' is not destiny before it happens. In fact, we are taught in the Jewish tradition that negative prophesies can be changed, but positive prophesies always come true.

But once something occurs, it is always Destiny. With a capital 'D'. Life is 100% Destiny in retrospect. Once something occurs, it never, ever would have happened any other way.

The events that we experience are always personal to us. Once they happen, they are 'meant to be' — an essential part of our life-journey, the Spiritual Learning-Journey that we call 'Life'. At the same time, these events are a separate-yet-connected story-line with the other people and agents that contribute to those events.

So coming back to God's words, what God is saying here is: "I see the suffering of the people, and I remember them, and I'm going to keep my covenant with them. I *also see* what this nation of Egypt and this Pharaoh have done to them. That was their choice. *They did not have to be the agents of suffering*. That was a choice they made."

There is a separation, philosophically, to be drawn between the 'life-message' experiences that happen to us in our life-journey, and the people or 'culprits' that are the agents of our life-experiences. This is what Joseph tried to explain to his brothers when they were reunited twenty years after they had sold him into bondage.

Joseph said, "I forgive you for what you did. You need to reconcile that now between yourselves—'How could we have done such a thing? How could we have done that to our father and our brother? How could we have done that before God? How did we do that in terms of our own character?'

"But as far as me," Joseph explained, "I was sent here as part of a Divine plan. I was sent here to save us."

And this is what Mordecai tells Esther in the Purim story: "If God wants to save the Jewish people from the evil plot of Haman, God will find a way with or without you. The only thing you need to decide is if it is *your destiny* to be the agent of salvation!"

So we learn from our Torah and heritage that there are two distinct and important aspects of each life-event:

> A) The agents of a life-event, and,
> B) The experience of a life-event,

and while they are connected, each of these elements must ultimately be understood as two separate conversations.

We must be able to see and draw this separation. It's a deep and profound idea, something which deserves tremendous contemplation.

It means that what happens to me in my life *has always happened to me for a reason*.

And it means that no one else is the 'author of my life'.

People often ask, "Why doesn't God talk to us?"

And the answer is: God is talking to us all the time! But God's mouthpiece is not a mouth like a human being's mouth. *God's mouthpiece is found in the flowing events of the world around us.* God's mouthpiece is *life and the experiences life presents to us* on a day-to-day and hour-to-hour and moment-to-moment level.

In this week's Torah portion, a very specific language is used to describe the Jewish people: "Nation."

Pharaoh says, "We have to find a way to deal with this Nation of Israel." Pharaoh calls us a *Nation.*

And then when God sends Moshe to Egypt, God says, "I've heard the suffering of *My Nation.*"

The term in the Torah for the Jewish people is "Nation."
We are not a religion.
We are a Nation.

We are a people with a <u>Language</u> and with a <u>Land</u> and with a <u>Legal Constitution</u>. That Constitution is found in our Torah, and elucidated in our Mishna and our Talmud and all the timeless works of Jewish Law that we derive from them!

It was Napoleon who famously recognized the Jewish people as a Nation, and said, "Look, enough of this idea of Nationhood business. Stop with the 'Nationhood'. Be a religion and be French. But give up this concept of Nationhood."

There's a reason the Romans renamed the land of Israel "Philistina": Because there was a Nationhood that they wanted to erase! They were not bothered or threatened by the religion itself…

So how did the Jewish people become a religion?

Well, when you take away a People's land, scatter them around the world, and deny them their collective rights, all that is left for them is to hold on to are *their Traditions.* And yes, the world calls that 'practicing of Spiritual Tradition' "religion". But the Jewish people are much more than that!!

Because in our prayers we've been praying for 2,000 years *without break, without pause, since the moment we left Israel, we have been praying to return to Israel and Jerusalem!!* We pray for it three times a day in our daily prayers. We pray for it in our after-blessings when we dine, whether it's the Birkat HaMazon, the longer after-blessing, or the Al HaMichiya, the shorter after-blessing.

We have never for a moment in 2,000 years given up our claim to our homeland.
We have never for a moment stopped talking to God in the language of our people.

The tragedy of it is that we have still somehow forgotten that we are a *Nation*. And this collective forgetfulness has brought great confusion into our lives and into the lives of the Nations of the World that seek to understand us.

Let's flash-forward to the 21st Century, and take a moment to consider some issues that regularly arise in current events. It seems that perhaps God is challenging us once again with world-events and evolutions no less profound than the days of ancient Egypt. He is prodding us and poking us to look deep within, and *remember who we are.*

For well more than a decade, we cannot get through a few weeks or months without the political and security shifts in the world creating a 'blowback' on both the Israeli and diaspora Jewish communities; and these blowback moments cause a tremendous amount of pain and confusion for a lot of Jewish people around the world.

One common result of this blowback, in the USA in particular, is a terminology called "Israel Firsters" as a now 'kosher' subject and language of debate in mainstream politics. On National Public Radio (NPR) in the USA and major news networks, as well as in popular blogs, senior political commentators and pundits in Western media have been using a very hurtful term called "Israel Firsters" to refer to Jews.

The expression 'Israel-Firsters' is used to question (or outright state) that Jews have a dual loyalty, wherein our greatest loyalty is not to America or Canada or England or France or to wherever our Western country of citizenship may be. It implies that Jewish patriotism is questionable, and that our first loyalty is to Israel; that the Jewish people will readily sell out their Western host countries for Israel. Both the Simon Wiesenthal Center and the Anti-Defamation League have gone on record to state that this terminology is tremendously anti-Semitic.

And the question is how to respond to this accusation, which has now entered mainstream discourse? If we stop to think about this terminology and it's claim about the Jewish people, how should we react? And as loyal Western citizens who have faced this type of attack over our past 2,000 years of exile, the other deeper question is: Why do such attacks happen to us? And why is it happening again?

Because you know what? The question of Israel-Firsters and dual loyalty? That's not a question! That's a reality!! That's something we should be proud of!! We don't need to defend ourselves against that questioning of our values! We need to declare it!

Do you think that if America went to war against Ireland, that Irish Americans wouldn't be upset, wouldn't have a problem with that?! Really?! You bet they would!

Do you think that if America went to war against Italy, that Italians wouldn't have a problem with that?! You bet they would!

Do you think that if America went to war against England, that naturalized English people wouldn't have a problem with that?! Of course they would!

But if you're dealing with just a Christian American, that is a different conversation.   You would say, "Well, would they suddenly turn against America in the name of the New Testament?" That would be disturbing and wrong! Because *a religion shouldn't be a reason to turn against your country*.

And that is why Jewish *religious law* requires a person to honor the laws of his or her host-nation! Judaism has an actual law,

Dinah d'Malchuta Dinah, that God demands that we must respect the laws of the lands we live in. This is something that God expects us to abide by and respect! That's pretty awesome.

So to question if the Jewish religion would place Jews in conflict with America if America were ever to turn against Israel, that's only a question if you define Judaism as a religion. And from a religious perspective, our Torah expects us to honor the laws of the country we live in.

But if we remember that we are a Nation and that Israel is our Native Homeland, well then of course we are entitled to the same pride as an Irish person or an Italian or an English expat! We are entitled to the same Native National Pride as anyone else!! Because that's what America is made up of!

America is a place which has gathered in, and is made up of, all kinds of people from all kinds of Nations! And you bet if America went to war against one of those nations, that people who still call themselves Irish or Italian after four generations, you bet they would be bent out of shape about it!

And so, instead of having to apologize and invoke the Simon Wiesenthal Center and the ADL, we should just be saying, "You're damn straight! 'Cause that's my Nation, too. *Those are my Roots.* And that's what America is made of."

Next Current Events question: Over the past several years, the leader of the Palestinian Authority, known alternatively as both "Abu Mazen" and "Mahmoud Abbas", has taken on a hardened and firm public position that has put Israel on edge, creating wide debate among many Jewish people around the world, raising a really big question mark in the minds and hearts of the global Jewish community.

He has repeatedly declared: *"Let me be perfectly clear: I will never, ever agree to recognize Israel as a **Jewish** state. You can call Israel a state which has a majority population of Jews. You can decide for yourselves as the State of Israel to make Judaism your national religion. But there's no such thing as a Jewish state because **Judaism is a religion, not a Nation**. There's no such thing as The Jewish **Nation**. And don't expect us to help create that fiction for you."*

Such painful, provocative words. But the question is: Are Mahmoud Abbas and his Palestinian Authority cohorts, who echo and repeat this claim and position again and again, correct?

Their position and vocal challenge to this subject of Jewish identity forces us, as Jewish people around the world, to search our Souls. They raise an *extremely* important question! Are we a "Nation"? Or are we merely a persecuted *religious* minority among many across the world, looking for a safe place to live? *It is a question we need to answer.*

And finally, our third Current Events question: The global campaign to erase Jewish history from Israel, led by the Palestinian Authority and confirmed repeatedly by UNESCO into a newly falsified global-education "reality". It is a crazy, mind-bending thing that the Palestinian Authority can suddenly claim that the Tomb of Rachel, Matriarch of the Jewish dynasty, is in fact not said tomb but rather an Islamic mosque. It is especially crazy, because all the books of *Muslim history* recognize the Tomb of Rachel to be *the Tomb of Rachel, Matriarch of the Jewish dynasty*! But what is entirely crazy is that UNESCO then votes to ratify this new, invented and politically driven rewriting of a 4,000 year old historical gravesite, that is so sacred to Jewish history and the Jewish people.

And what is heartbreakingly crazy, is that once UNESCO becomes coopted into such a cynical distortion of historical truth and current realities, the positions of UNESCO become mainstreamed into global educational texts, from Ivy League Universities to grade-school world-history. And the truth of Judaism is suddenly erased from "factual" world-history.

Yes, Jewish history is being written out of the books, with the rubber-stamp of "authority" from a morally bankrupt and hijacked U.N., right before our modern, enlightened eyes.

This gross falsification-of-history campaign was brought into sharp contrast recently, when US President Donald Trump decided to formally recognize Jerusalem as the Capital of Israel and the Jewish People (he noted both the *current political reality* of the State of Israel having chosen it's Capital, as well as *ancient Jewish history* in his recognition speech and accompanying Presidential Proclamation).

Did you see the reactions around the world?? Did you see the hand-wringing around President Trump's apparently *'provocative act'*?

Seriously? Has anyone been at a Reform, Conservative, Reconstructionist, or Orthodox Jewish wedding at any time over the past 2,000 years (including today!)? Remember when we ALL break a glass as we remember JERUSALEM??

Not 'Israel'.   JERUSALEM.

And let's not even get into our three-times-a-day prayers for the last 2,000 years, or the Jewish Grace After Meals, and the countless times we remember and pray for JERUSALEM!

So 'Yes', world: *Jerusalem is the Capital of the Jewish People.* And it should cause us — the Jewish people across the world — great consternation to hear and see nations across the world wringing their hands when the US President says this out loud.

It should alarm us terribly that these same world leaders *do not wring their hands* and are *very comfortable and silent* when the Palestinian leadership declares at the United Nations that the Jewish people have *no history in Jerusalem*!

Did you know that since the very beginning of Oslo, Yasser Arafat, Mahmoud Abbas, and the Palestinian Authority have consistently claimed and insisted that the Temple Mount is not in fact the Temple Mount, and that no Jewish Temple was ever in Jerusalem? It is crazy! We have taken it in stride year after year, and pretended that it doesn't mean anything. We have chosen to ignore that the people with whom we are negotiating peace have an *open agenda* to erase 3,500 years of Jewish history!

Did you know that in 2011 the Palestinian Authority was granted full membership in UNESCO?   Since then, the Palestinian Authority has succeeded in the following:

1) The Tomb of Rachel our Matriarch has been redefined and declared to be an ancient Muslim Mosque
2) The Tomb of Rachel our Matriarch has been redefined and declared to be "an integral part of the Occupied Palestinian Territory"
3) Israel has been formally condemned for engaging in activities that are "destructive to the *Muslim* status of this site"
4) The Cave of Machpela, the tomb of the Jewish people's Patriarchs and Matriarchs has been redefined and declared to be a Muslim site
5) The Cave of Machpela has been redefined and declared to be "an integral part of the Occupied Palestinian Territory"
6) Israel has been cited for engaging in activities that are "destructive to the *Muslim* status of this site"
7) UNESCO has formally ruled that the Temple Mount has nothing to do with Judaism, and that Israel is actively destroying this ancient *Muslim* historical site

The PA is able to do this because despite the fact that *ALL ancient Muslim texts* (along with all other historical texts) recognize these sites to be the *ancient Jewish sites* that they are, UNESCO has not made these decisions based upon historical research! They made their decisions based upon member-votes, and the majority of their members are hostile to Israel!

What does this mean as regards global historical education? Let me explain:

UNESCO is the **U**nited **N**ations **E**ducational, **S**cientific and **C**ultural **O**rganization. Its declared purpose is *"To contribute to peace and security by promoting* *international collaboration through **educational, scientific, and cultural reforms** in order to increase **universal respect for justice**, the rule of law, and human rights along with fundamental freedom proclaimed in the United Nations Charter."*

*"A World Heritage Site is a landmark or area which is selected by UNESCO as having cultural, historical, scientific or other form of significance, and **is legally protected by international treaties**. The sites are judged important to the collective interests of humanity."*

*"To be selected, a World Heritage Site must be an already classified landmark, unique in some respect as a geographically and **historically identifiable place having special cultural or physical significance**. It may signify a remarkable accomplishment of humanity, and **serve as evidence of our intellectual history** on the planet."*

*"The program catalogues, names, and conserves sites of outstanding cultural or natural importance to **the common culture and heritage of humanity. 193 state parties have ratified the convention**, making it one of **the most widely recognized international agreements** and the world's most popular cultural program."*

How can it be that a world organization whose purpose is to preserve those sites which are of historical significance all over the world, instead actively acts to erase 3,500 years of Jewish history (which is also part of Christian history, and yes, also part of 1,500 years of Muslim history)?! It's such a painful, mind-boggling thing…

So how do we react, as members of the Jewish people around the world? What should our reaction be? And why, we need to ask, *why why why* are we being challenged like this?

It is not enough to just look at the Palestinian Authority and point a finger at them. Just like in the times of our Torah, it was not enough to simply blame Pharaoh and the Egyptians for our fate, or for Joseph to blame his brothers for his destiny.

We have to look at ourselves. We have to look at our relationship with our Spiritual heritage. We have to look at our personal and collective relationships with God.

And here I want to tell you two very important, personal stories…

> *Many years ago, when I was working down in Wall Street, I grabbed a taxi. It was pouring rain that day. I was wearing a rain coat and I was wearing a hat. And I got in this cab and it was really like a little mosque. It was so full of religious elements in this cab, and I thought: Wow, what an opportunity I have here! I've got a religiously devout Muslim cab driver, and for the first time that I can remember, there's no way for him to know that I'm Jewish. My kippah is covered by my hat. My tzitzit, my fringes, are covered by my coat. What an opportunity to ask questions and hear from the other side how he feels! What a great*

opportunity to hear from the 'other party' without him feeling like he has to be an apologist or defensive because he's talking to a Jewish person!

And so I said, "Excuse me, sir. Do you mind if I ask you some questions about something that I'm trying to understand?"

He said, "Sure, my friend. What is it?"

I said, "Can you explain to me what's going on in Israel between the Jews and the Muslims?"

And he said to me, "You mean 'Palestine.'"

And I said, "OK, Palestine. What's going on there? What's all the fighting about? Where is it all going?"

And he looked me dead in the eye in his rearview mirror and he said, "Don't worry, my friend. We will win."

I said, "You'll win? How do you know? You sound so certain!"

He said, "I <u>am</u> certain."

I said, "But how can you be certain? I read the papers every day. It looks completely up-in-the-air! It's so confusing! This-one-and-that-one, this-one-and-that-one!

It goes back and forth every day! It doesn't seem like there's any clear winner or loser..."

And my driver told me: "I want to teach you something, my friend, and I want you to hear my words and bring them to your heart and never, ever forget them." He said, "When you listen to the Jewish people speak, they talk to you about signing accords, pieces of paper, U.N. Resolutions, American treaties." He said, "All of these documents are written by human beings. But when you listen to the Muslim people speak, you will hear us talk about the <u>word of God</u>. We are concerned with that which God has said, and therefore that which must be true."

And my driver concluded: "I can assure you my kind friend, bring these words to your heart: In the history of humankind, it will never, ever happen that the words and papers of human beings will somehow overrule the words of God. And so I tell you, my friend, <u>we will win</u>."

And I was *so humbled* by the faith of this person. Because what he was saying is true. Not the part about who will win or lose, God forbid, but the idea of *connecting with the word of God*. The idea of remembering where we come from and not being embarrassed by our Heritage, by our Spirituality, by our Roots, and by *where we come from...*

Many years ago, I was on a flight down to South Beach to visit a friend for the weekend, and I'm talking to the guy next to me. We get to talking about where we're from, and I say, "I'm from Israel."

He looks over and says, "You don't sound Israeli."

"No," I said. "We just moved there a few years ago. I actually grew up in Connecticut and I lived in New Jersey after that."

And he looks at me again and he asks, "So why would you move to Israel?"

And I said to him, "Well, let me ask you a question. What about you? What are your roots? Where do you come from?"

He says, "Oh, me? I'm Irish."

And I ask, "Oh, wow. You were born in Ireland?"

He says, "No."

"Was your father born in Ireland?"

"No."

"Your grandfather?"

"Nope."

"So who?"

"Well, actually, my great grandparents came over here."

I said, "Wow. But yet, you still call yourself Irish?"

And he answered, "Well, I am Irish."

And then I told him: "That's exactly the point! Even though you've been here for four generations, you still know your roots! You still know who you are. But when you talk to Jewish people in America, most of them will (sadly) tell you, 'I'm an American'. Because we have forgotten our roots. And I've moved back to Israel so that my children will become reconnected with their roots."

What my new Irish acquaintance could not imagine, is that there is a big, big difference between an Israeli who makes *'yeridah'*, who moves to the Diaspora, and a Diaspora Jew who has never connected with Israel.

An Israeli who lives in America, even a second or third generation Israeli, he or she possesses an unshakable sense of **Nationhood**. But a Jewish person who was born and raised in the Diaspora can never fully know or comprehend that powerful sense of rootedness. Even if they visit Israel every year, and own a vacation apartment in Jerusalem, it still isn't the same.

Believe me, if you are a Diaspora Jew reading this, and doubt my words, I would have doubted them too, before I moved back to

Israel. But I am telling you, once you experience Judaism as *Nationhood* on the level of daily living, a power inside you *is restored* that is greater than anything you can imagine.

Judaism is **not** a Religion.

Judaism is a **Nationhood**.

We are a Nation with a *Spiritual doctrine, a Spiritual orientation, discipline and mission* to carry out within the world community.

But we are a **Nation**.

We must open ourselves up to what is happening to us in life, to the conversation God is having with us. We must open our hearts, and seek the lessons to be learned from what we are going through.

So let's return to the signs Moshe was given by God, and their incredibly beautiful, powerful meaning.

The message of the Burning Bush is this:

God is teaching Moshe: "I'm not looking to destroy anyone. And yes, your people may be in the midst of a fire right now. But they're not going to be consumed by it. Look at the prayers and Faith that have emerged from their trials! Look at the power and endurance of Spirit they have found in themselves."

Even in the fires of life, even in the midst of hardship, there is always hope. This life is not about destruction. The fiery trials of life are not meant to destroy us, but rather to increase our wonder and reveal our indestructible power! This is the wonder of God's world. This is the wonder of us as human beings, and particularly as the Jewish Nation: *That we can burn, but we will endure.*

The message of the snake and of the leprous hand is this:
That while, yes, we may go through hardship and we might witness destruction, the same God who brought those tests upon us will bring about salvation. There is always hope. *Redemption is the final chapter of our story.*

Pharaoh's magicians are able to replicate the first few plagues and turn their staffs into snakes. They're able to effect *destruction*. What they're not able to do is *turn the snake back into a staff*. They can't turn the water that's been turned into blood, *back into water again*. They're able to repeat the first few plagues, but *they can't reverse them*.

God's message in the signs was to show the Jewish people: "I know it's bad, *but* **We** *can make this right again.* **You** *can make this right again. It will be alright again.*"

Redemption is the final chapter of our story.

And the message of the cup of water from the nile turning into blood is this:
Sometimes, as human beings, we feel so lost and broken that we fear that God does not see what we are going through. We feel abandoned and alone.

The Jews in Egypt felt this way. "No, you don't know how bad it is. Pharaoh's been throwing our babies into the sea. First, he tried to get the midwives to kill them at birth and tell us that they were stillborn. *He tried to hide his crimes*. When that didn't work he said, 'Throw their newborns in the sea. The sea will cover up my crimes and my evil.' *No one knows what's happening here.* You don't know the evil!"

So God said, "Scoop up some of the water and throw it on the land. When it turns to blood, revealing the dark secret of the sea, *they will know that I see how bad it is*."

"I see your pain, always, and I understand how bad it is. And when I tell you it will get better, it's from a point of infinite understanding."

And the message to *us* when Moshe comes to Pharaoh the first time, and Pharaoh refuses to listen and things get worse, is this:
When you know the Truth is on your side, don't give up. Things *will* get better. *Goodness wins.*

Finally, the message of the Jewish slaves challenging Moshe and Aharon, but never doubting God, is this:

When we go through the hardest times, it's sometimes because it is from that place that we will find our greatest strength. All of life is a gift, and all of life is love, and even in life's hardest moments there is a lesson for us to discover, and an opportunity for us to grow. *But it can only be unlocked by challenging our reality, while never losing our faith in God, or in the Trueness of our Journey.*

When we hear the Palestinians start saying, "Judaism is a religion. There's no such thing as a Jewish Nation." Instead of saying, *"Hey, that's not nice,"* or reacting with the handwringing and the tepidness we have until now, we should should look them in the eye and tell them: "I don't see how it will help further interests in the future of the Palestinian people, to stick a thumb in the eye of the Faith and Holy texts of *every Christian and every Jew in the world*. Because the Bible disagrees with you, Mahmoud Abbas! The Bible disagrees with you, UNESCO!"

The Bible is pretty explicit. Pharaoh knew we were a Nation. God identifies us as a Nation.

And so much of our own confusion in terms of our right to this land, is getting in the way of our sharing it with others with love. And yes, it is our right to share it, and we would love to share it!

There's no problem from the view of Jewish National Law (our Torah) in sharing our land with others who have no other home to go to! But it has to be clear that it is **ours to share, and not anyone else's to take!!**

We are in **our land** of Israel. And in our land, we can choose to provide a state or an autonomous region for anyone we choose, whether Bahai or Beduin or Palestinian. But it's for the Jewish Nation, **it is the Jewish Nation's right,** to afford that space.

Our Torah tells us right here in the time of ancient Egypt to never ever forget what it was like to be a homeless people in a strange land. HaShem is demanding of us that we remember the good years when we had the area of Goshen *to rule over ourselves autonomously* under the good Pharaoh in the time of Joseph.

We have no problem sharing our land with other people and granting other people areas to live autonomously with their own self-governance (so long as they are peaceful and respectful towards us, as we were towards Pharaoh and Egypt).

Nor can we forget that ***it is ours to give***.

And so the hardship of these Current Events for our People, the hardship of these years, the hardship of the questions that are being raised at this time in history towards the Jewish Nation and especially to the Jewish people of the Diaspora, is to *remember who you are. Remember what you are.* **You are a Nation. This is your land. This is your Torah. This is your Birthright.**

We do not need to apologize for our National heritage.
We have so much to be proud of.
And it would be a gift to the world for us to *understand ourselves.*
Because only after we understand ourselves, will the world be able to understand us, too.

_____

The message of this week's reflections on the Torah portion, for each of us on an individual level, Jewish and non-Jewish, is to understand that every hardship and every trial that we go through is meant to teach us something, or lead us to greater strength and growth. *The events in our lives are never about what 'someone is doing to us'. They are always a message for us.*

Each one of us is a Burning Bush.
Each one of us in our lives will face many struggles and many moments when we feel like we're being consumed.
But we're not.
Because the staff that turns into a snake when we lose our grip on it, when we seize it the right way, it will turn back into a staff and support us as we journey forward.

And the hand that seems so sick, in fact will become a healthy hand again as we take authorship over our own lives, and transform trials into strengths.

But most importantly, to understand that ultimately, even our pain that we think no one else sees… God sees it.

God sees us. And ultimately, HaShem, God, is in each and every one of our corners. Always.

Week 14: The Torah Portion of 'Va'eira'

The Godly Power to Heal

So here's an amazing Torah. Really, really cool.

During the second plague, in which God strikes Egypt with the Plague of Frogs, the Torah says:

וַיֵּט אַהֲרֹן אֶת־יָדוֹ עַל מֵימֵי מִצְרָיִם וַתַּעַל הַצְּפַרְדֵּעַ וַתְּכַס אֶת־אֶרֶץ מִצְרָיִם

"Aharon spread out his hand on the water of Egypt, and the frogs rose up and they covered the land of Egypt..."

וַיַּעֲשׂוּ־כֵן הַחַרְטֻמִּים בְּלָטֵיהֶם וַיַּעֲלוּ אֶת־הַצְפַרְדְּעִים עַל־אֶרֶץ מִצְרָיִם

"...and the Egyptian magicians were able to do the same thing through their sorcery, and they also raised up frogs upon the land of Egypt..."

וַיִּקְרָא פַרְעֹה לְמֹשֶׁה וּלְאַהֲרֹן וַיֹּאמֶר הַעְתִּירוּ אֶל־ה' וְיָסֵר הַצְפַרְדְּעִים מִמֶּנִּי וּמֵעַמִּי

"...and then Pharaoh called to Moshe and Aharon and said, 'Please appeal to HaShem and get these frogs off of me and off of my nation..." (Shemot 8:1-3)

And so here's the thing. If you notice, the Egyptian magicians were able to compound the trouble, but they couldn't reverse the trouble. Similarly, with the first plague, Moshe and Aharon turned the water of Egypt into blood. And Pharaoh's magicians were able to turn more water into blood, create more destruction, but they couldn't reverse it.

But let's think about it: What were the Egyptians proving by replicating the plague? Why would they want to bring *more frogs* into Egypt?! It's a plague! Here they are covered with frogs, and they're going to bring more frogs?! They want to show their ability to compound their trouble??

It's like a person who makes a mistake, and then, rather than admitting to their mistake, they are like, "Yeah, I meant to do that...". The person is so insecure that rather than owning their mistake, they try to cover it up. And sometimes they will repeat the same foolish action again, just to 'prove' that they really meant to do it! They'll do or say anything, rather than just admitting that they have made a mistake...

And here's where things get interesting in terms of the way that God is engaging the Egyptians and Pharaoh: Because while they can posture and pose all they want about how they are totally cool with the mess that is happening around them, when they want to undo the trouble *they can only do so by turning to HaShem*.

And Pharaoh is forced to acknowledge this. He sees his magicians compounding the problems, but immediately after their showmanship, we see Pharaoh turning to Moshe and Aharon saying, "Please appeal to God to reverse the problem, to relieve us of this trouble."

And that's the lesson that's going on here. That's what is important during these first few plagues. *What is important reaches beyond the plagues themselves, and is found in the lesson that they are teaching*. HaShem is teaching Pharaoh and his 'all-powerful' sorcerers that *Real Power* is not found in the power to destroy, but rather in the Power to Heal.

And we see this lesson being highlighted clearly in Moshe's words to Pharaoh regarding the event that is taking place. Moshe *doesn't* say to Pharaoh, "Now you have seen God's wonders through this plague!" Moshe *doesn't* highlight the plague and its destructiveness to Pharaoh. Rather, what does Moshe say?

וַיֹּאמֶר מֹשֶׁה לְפַרְעֹה הִתְפָּאֵר עָלַי לְמָתַי | אַעְתִּיר לְךָ וְלַעֲבָדֶיךָ וּלְעַמְּךָ לְהַכְרִית הַצְפַרְדְּעִים מִמְּךָ וּמִבָּתֶּיךָ רַק בַּיְאֹר תִּשָׁאַרְנָה

"Moshe said to Pharaoh: 'You name the time. Name a time. Any time you want for all the frogs to disappear and go back into the rivers.'"

וַיֹּאמֶר לְמָחָר

"And Pharaoh says, 'Tomorrow.'" (8:5-6)

"Tomorrow", Pharaoh says. Such an interesting answer. It's meaningful that Pharaoh chooses this answer, because it shows that Pharaoh is intrigued by Moshe's challenge that there is a Healing Power in the world, and that Moshe is prepared to prove the Presence of this Healing Power by having it manifest at *any time* of Pharaoh's choosing.

So Pharaoh chooses very carefully. He thinks, "Maybe Moshe is saying this because Moshe somehow knows that this plague is about to end anyway, for reasons having nothing to do with him, and he wants to fool me into thinking that the change that is about to take place is within his power." So Pharaoh wants to push it off a little bit, to make certain the plague was not about to end anyways. But he doesn't want to push it off too much because it is a plague, after all!

So Pharaoh picks a time that's far enough away to prove that it is happening 'on-demand' from a Higher Healing Power, but not too far away to overextend the suffering of himself and his people. And Moshe declares:

וַיֹּאמֶר כִּדְבָרְךָ לְמַעַן תֵּדַע כִּי-אֵין כַּה' אֱלֹקינוּ

"It will be exactly as you said! So you'll know there is no one like our God!" (8:6)

It's such a very deep and powerful message here that Moshe is teaching to Pharaoh: That the sign of HaShem's wonder is not so much in the plague, but rather in *God's ability to reverse the trouble*, to heal us from our troubles.

In fact, we see the same symbolism with every one of the *Simanim,* the initial signs, that HaShem had Moshe and Aharon perform before Pharaoh and his officers when they first arrived in Egypt with their message to let the Jewish people go. Consider the difference between the actions of Moshe and Aharon and the copying antics of the Egyptian sorcerers.

Aharon threw down his staff and it turned into a snake, but then he picked it up and turned it back into a staff. Pharaoh's magicians could only turn their staves into snakes; they could not reverse the process. And not only did Aharon's staff turn back into a staff, thereby undoing the bad, but before it returned to a staff it consumed the other staves-turned-into-snakes of the sorcerers, and then still turned back into a staff! It was able to consume all of the trouble and then return to its original safe, perfect, non-threatening state.

Similarly, when HaShem gave Moshe the sign of *Tzara'at*, the leprosy, the power was not as much in Moshe's hand turning leprous; rather, it was in seeing his had turn healthy again! All of HaShem's signs, all of the wonders, reflect this Healing Majesty of HaShem.

Even with all of the plagues, the emphasis of the Torah is not placed upon the actual afflictions themselves and all the drama in Egypt that each plague certainly caused. Rather, the emphasis in focused upon HaShem's ability to reverse the trouble, and Pharaoh's evolving appeals to Moshe to turn to HaShem for salvation (Pharaoh goes from saying "Who is this God?! I do not know this God!", to later openly confessing his own sins as the cause for the suffering upon him, to finally, at the tenth plague, asking for a Bracha, a blessing, from Moshe!)

I learned from Rav Rachmiel, a teacher of mine from Ohr Sameyach, that the Hebrew names for Mitzrayim (Egypt) and Mitzrim (Egyptians) derive from the Hebrew word *Meitzar* (narrow straights, a place of confinement & distress). And therefore this ancient nation of Egypt symbolizes a people who are imprisoned by their behaviors, who are stuck in their ways. They are confined by their own habits, by their their own limited boundaries, and they can't break out. They symbolize the person who is stuck in his or her own self-destructive patterns.

Every person has the ability to destroy. Destroying is easy. Even babies can break things. And as we grow and mature, if we are not thoughtful in the way we live, we run the risk of getting stuck in certain habits and behavior patterns — self-destructive, non-productive, confining patterns. And sometimes, God forbid, a person can reach a point where he or she is unable to free themselves from these habits, when reversing their life-patterns is no longer a simple matter of choice.

But there is always hope! There is always a pathway by which we may reverse our patterns of self-destruction and unhealthy living! When we reach that 'Mitzri' level, God forbid, we need to turn to HaShem and tap into that Godly Healing Power that is invested within our world and within ourselves. It is a Healing Power rooted in our Faith and understanding in the ways of HaShem, which He has invested in us. It is the power of Yehudah, Yehudi, the Jewish Spirit to say: *"Tzadka Mimeini!!"* To get up and say, *"I can turn this around right now!!"*

How did Pharaoh rule? Pharaoh ruled with fear. Pharaoh was all about: "I see these strong people, and I see a threat." And rather than harnessing the positive energy of the Jewish people who had always lived peacefully in Egypt, he took a negative approach of *force* and *violence* in order to feed into his *fears.*

If he would have only looked into Egypt's own recent history! If he would have only looked at his own royal records! He would have seen the good the Jews had done for Egypt, and how the previous Pharaoh had harnessed the blessings of Yosef for all of Egypt's benefit. He would have seen the healing, flourishing Power of HaShem, if he only would have been motivated by Love and Respect instead of Fear and Control. Instead of slavery, he could have harnessed the positive energy of this blessed Nation of Israel…

Don't forget: When Yosef was a servant in Potiphar's house, Potiphar saw that Yosef was blessed and didn't feel threatened by Yosef, but instead elevated him in his home; the result was great blessing! Similarly, when Yosef was thrown in prison the head of the prison saw that Yosef was blessed by God and elevated him in the prisons. And when the previous Pharaoh realized that Yosef had special gifts, the first Pharaoh elevated Yosef — also to a result of great blessing! But this new Pharaoh, rather than *elevating the light* around him, he rules through fear. He rules through Destructive Force. And when it doesn't work, he increases that force...

But he made a mistake. Because he increased the force to such a degree that he began taking lives. He began killing children. And that darkness — reaching a place of such a total shutdown of his own morality and decency — ultimately brought upon his people *Makat Bechorot,* the death of the firstborn children of Egypt.

The story of Pharaoh is the story of bad habits turned into destructive, addictive behaviors. And it is a tragic example of falling into a dangerous false-illusion that we can fix our world through Force and Fear.
Or fix our children through force or fear...
Or fix our friendships this way...
Or fix ourselves this way...
And indeed, this paradigm is false.

Love heals. Kindness heals. Faith heals. *Optimism heals.* And *Simcha* — a battlecry of Unconditional Joy in our world, breaks through all sealed doors!!

We have such great, great, Godly healing power invested in us as human beings. But to tap into that Healing Power, we have to get to know HaShem. We have to get to know how HaShem works, and recognize that HaShem shows his greatest power not through sending a storm, but rather through returning the sunshine to us after the storm. We have to get to know that the Jewish day starts with nightfall, but concludes with daylight.

Goodness Wins.

We also need to exercise caution. We need to understand, and respect, and remain humble to our own frailties as human beings. Because fear can paralyze us, God forbid. And anger can blind us, God forbid. And ruling through force can seduce us, God forbid; but it will never redeem us. Its fruits are always poisonous, if eaten from for too long.

And this is what happened to Pharaoh. A man whose habits, driven by fear, led him into a deep addiction to power and control. Pharaoh is the alcoholic CEO who cannot see that the iron grip of his vice is destroying everything around him, his company and his family. He is the powerful executive whose closest advisors can no longer reach him, and can no longer talk him down from his headstrong run towards the edge of a fateful cliff.

When God "hardens Pharaoh's heart", the Torah is teaching a lesson to us all. The Torah is cautioning us that as human beings, poor choices repeated too often can slowly rob us of our free will. A bad habit is the loss of a bit of free will. And an addiction, God forbid, is sometimes a total loss of freedom-of-choice.

Makat Bechorot, the death of the first-born children of Egypt, is an agonizing symbol of the vast tragedy that comes from a human life driven by negativity and unchecked passions. And this tragic lesson of the Death of the First-Born of Egypt is so central to Jewish wisdom that we bind it to us in the Teffilin we put on every morning during our morning payers; the story is one of the four meditations inscribed within our Teffilin. The story of the death of the first-born also holds a central place in our Heritage Holiday of Passover. And finally, we reflect upon it in our morning prayers every day, right before the Silent Meditation of Shemoneh Esreh.

The tenth plague is a siren-call of caution.
We can get lost.
Our hearts can become hardened.
We can get to the point where we God forbid lose our connection to the Healing Power of HaShem that flows through our world and flows through each and every one of us.

Importantly, the Torah highlights that HaShem performed *Makat Bechorot,* and no one else. Because sometimes when a person refuses to learn, God forbid it can reach a point where the *Deen*, the judgment, becomes final. But that *Deen* is only for HaShem to decide. No one else can place that judgment upon another human being. No-one else has the right to give up on another human being. It is for God to decide when to 'bring the hammer down' upon a person who has fallen too far into darkness. It is *for us* to follow God's example of never giving up on another person, just as God sought to save Pharaoh from himself through nine other miraculous, illustrative plagues. Our takeaway lesson is found in the first nine plagues and their reversals: That even the most supernatural calamities in life can be reversed by a simple and humble act of prayer.

Pharaoh, our tragic antihero, went too far in his negative approach to life. And his friends were enablers, hooked on the same drug of arrogance and power that Pharaoh was. He got his reassurance from his own magicians creating more of the same trouble—turning more water into blood, bringing more frogs upon Egypt.

But the message Moshe and Aharon sought to bring to Pharaoh was that he needed to rule according to HaShem's example. He had to look to HaShem. And that power of HaShem is *the Power to undo the damage, and the Power to Heal*. The message to Pharaoh was:

"Undo the damage.

Rule through goodness.

Harness your power.

Break out of those unhealthy boundaries.

Don't be a Mitzri, because indulging in your weaknesses is bringing you and your people to a point of total self-destruction.

True Power is not manifest in the power to do harm.

Godly Power is manifest in our human ability to heal ourselves and the world around us.

Life is sacred.

And Goodness Wins."

We should all be blessed to see and to know that the example of HaShem's power for us, the message of our Torah, is that we each have a great Healing Power within us. And this power is found in our ability to transcend our routine habits and aspire to greater goodness, each and every day.

We exercise our Godliness when we don't submit to our habits, when we don't succumb to our boundaries, when we don't repeat our mistakes in an effort to justify them and to show that we meant *'to do it all along'*.   Rather, we show our Godliness when we stop, harness, turn around and shine — with a relentless joy and faith in ourselves, and in the people and world around us.

Week 15: The Torah Portion of 'Bo'

The Glory of Success, The Glory of Failure

This week's Torah portion examines the amazing culmination of a fascinating contrast in personalities, in personal stories, between Moshe and Pharaoh. And it's really a very Zen contrast, a presentation of a very Taoist concept, providing us with two opposite approaches to life: One is a person who tries to claim honor, to claim respect and to claim success through force vs. another who earns honor and earns success, enjoys honor and enjoys success through alignment.

The contrast between these two pathways of life is illuminated in our Torah portion, regarding the aspiration for success and how we get there, and the behaviors that produce true leadership and true power.

Alignment vs. Force.
Here we go…

Pharaoh, of course, represents Force. And Moshe in turn represents Alignment. And we see the outcomes of each approach resolving themselves in the most beautiful illustration in this week's Parshah.

One of the very difficult aspects of the story of the Exodus is the constant repetition of God saying He is going to "harden Pharaoh's heart". We see it right away in the opening of this Torah portion, when God says: "I'm going to harden his heart, and through that I'm going to do wonders."

This repeating expression raises a very uncomfortable question for us. It provokes us. It upsets us. After all, it seems very cynical and unfair, this idea of HaShem hardening peoples' hearts in order to do wonders. It doesn't really fit with the concept of God that we all like to imagine for ourselves.

And I'm always kind of fascinated by this question, when people get upset and say, "God can't do that! It's not fair!"

My first thought is always, "Well, um, actually. Yeah, God can do that. God can do whatever God wants. This is God's world. God is the Creator, and the paintbrush is in His hand..."

The indignance that we have as human beings when we hear this story told — and we all feel it — is really fascinating. Because that powerful feeling inside of us is a reflection, on a deep level, of how fair God usually is in our perception, and just how much order and how much sensibility there is in our world. It demonstrates how much we appreciate and defend this basic fundament of free will and freedom-of-choice that we've come to expect from God; that is so constant and fundamental in our day-to-day journey with God, and in our relationship with the world that God has given us.

Parshat Bo opens with this provocative idea, when HaShem says to Moshe:

וַיֹּאמֶר ה' אֶל־מֹשֶׁה בֹּא אֶל־פַּרְעֹה כִּי־אֲנִי הִכְבַּדְתִּי אֶת־לִבּוֹ וְאֶת־לֵב עֲבָדָיו לְמַעַן שִׁתִי אֹתֹתַי אֵלֶּה בְּקִרְבּוֹ

"I want you to come to Pharaoh because I have hardened his heart and the heart of his servants so that I can do more of my wonders in his midst." (Shemot 10:1)

But what if the hardening of his heart is not about taking away Pharaoh's free will, but in fact is about giving Pharaoh the ability to maintain free will? Because really — what kind of a human being could go toe-to-toe with God with all of these crazy wonders going on?! What kind of a person has the strength to play chess with God??

Pharaoh needs the help, Pharaoh needs a boost of Divine strength, in order to continue to maintain his free will. And that's what God is giving him.

We actually see clear evidence of this only a few pasukim later, a few passages later. We see Moses coming to warn Pharaoh about the coming plague of locusts. And after Moshe issues the warning, Pharaoh's servants turn to him and it says:

וַיֹּאמְרוּ עַבְדֵי פַרְעֹה אֵלָיו עַד־מָתַי יִהְיֶה זֶה לָנוּ לְמוֹקֵשׁ שַׁלַּח אֶת־הָאֲנָשִׁים וְיַעַבְדוּ אֶת־ה' אֱלֹקֵיהֶם הֲטֶרֶם תֵּדַע כִּי אָבְדָה מִצְרָיִם

"Pharaoh's servants say to him, 'How long is this going to continue? Let them go and serve HaShem, their God. Don't you realize that Egypt is being destroyed?'" (10:7)

And here's the key thing: A few passages prior we were told that God hardened the hearts of both Pharaoh and his servants. Yet we find them responding to events differently, making different choices. Pharaoh's servants are saying to Pharaoh: "Let them go serve God. You're destroying Egypt." And Pharaoh is refusing to let the Jewish people go free.

We see that this hardening of the heart is not taking away freedom of choice, but is in fact preserving the ability of people *to continue to make their own choices*. Both Pharaoh's heart and his servants hearts were hardened, but they made different, opposite choices!   Therefore, Pharaoh's decision not to let the Jewish people go, not to concede to God, is a choice *he's making on his own*. He has been given the strength to continue to decide for himself.

Now, that being said, what's God intent when he tells Moshe "so that I can broadcast My wonders"?

The answer is that ultimately we see God's wonder in this world in two ways.

Open your hearts...

The first way is as follows: We see God's wonder in the idea — the phenomena — of *Alignment*.

Spiritual Alignment manifests in a person who learns how to align their will with HaShem's will, their will with God's will, a person who is able to find that groove and find their place within the spiritual flow of life.

A natural success flows from that space. There's a natural harmony that surrounds that person and that attracts other people to that person. It's a harmony that begets success and manifests a natural, sweet and magnetically attractive leadership.

Moshe's question to HaShem was actually the opposite of ours: "Why are you giving Pharaoh free will? Why would you give him free will? Why didn't you just knock this guy down?"

And God says, "No. I maintain his free will because it's important that people see the wonder of My world. That a person with the free will to go head-to-head against the values of God, ultimately that kind of arrogance, that kind of aggression, that kind of ego, it will beget its own destruction. There is a natural order to the world. There is a Spiritual, self-correcting balance to the world.

Not only will you see my wonder and my ability to bless you to succeed — you, Moses, who never imagined yourself as a leader. But you will also see the wonder in watching how an arrogant leader, a man who has everything, can destroy everything simply through his own arrogance, and through his own aggression, and through his own ego."

This Torah portion provide us with such a deep, stark contrast, as we witness two opposite manifestations — one of *alignment* and one of *force* — resolving themselves as mirrors to one another.

We see the wonder — God Himself calls it "a wonder" — of seeing evil destroy itself.

And we also witness the wonder of seeing humbleness manifest itself.

Remember, back in the Torah portion of Shemot, when Moses says to God, "You've chosen the wrong guy"!

וַיֹּאמֶר מֹשֶׁה אֶל־ה' בִּי אֲדֹ־נָי לֹא אִישׁ דְּבָרִים אָנֹכִי גַּם מִתְּמוֹל גַּם מִשִּׁלְשֹׁם גַּם מֵאָז דַּבֶּרְךָ אֶל־עַבְדֶּךָ

"God, I'm the most ineloquent person in the world, so not a leader, and it's not from yesterday, not from the day before, not from the day you spoke to me..."

כִּי כְבַד־פֶּה וּכְבַד לָשׁוֹן אָנֹכִי

"…I am a person who stumbles in his speech."

וַיֹּאמֶר ה' אֵלָיו מִי שָׂם פֶּה לָאָדָם אוֹ מִי־יָשׂוּם אִלֵּם אוֹ חֵרֵשׁ אוֹ פִקֵּחַ אוֹ
עִוֵּר הֲלֹא אָנֹכִי ה'

*"And God replies to him: 'Who gives a man a mouth? Who makes
a person mute or deaf? Who gives a person sight or blindness?
Am I not God?"*
(Exodus 4:10-11)

In both cases, we witness the 'Divine Mechanics' of this world. The Torah illustrates for us the karma, so to speak, of alignment in contrast to force. We see It manifest in the harmony of a person who aligns, and also we see God's wonder in the natural correction that takes place when evil manifests itself. We see it on both levels.

This is the contrast between Pharaoh and Moshe. In this Parsha we really see each of them hitting the full stride of what they represent in their contrast of personalities, this contrast of pathways.

Pharaoh can't let go. He can't acknowledge a God bigger than him. Whenever he talks about God, Pharaoh constantly says, "Go serve HaShem, *your* God." He always refers to HaShem as *their* God. He can never admit that HaShem is just HaShem. It's never "Hashem, God." It's always "your God."

After the warning for the locusts, when his servants say to Pharaoh, "What are you crazy? You're gonna destroy Egypt." So he calls Moshe and Aaron back in and he says to them,

וַיֹּאמֶר אֲלֵהֶם לְכוּ עִבְדוּ אֶת־ה' אֱלֹקיכֶם
"Go serve Hashem, your God..." (10:8)

Not Hashem as God, but Hashem as *your* God. "I have my God, and I am myself Pharaoh—I am a god. But you can go serve *your* God."

מִי וָמִי הַהֹלְכִים
"...but who's going?" (10:8)

He puts limitations on it. He says: "You can serve God, but let's agree to the terms because really that's something that I need to decide here."

Here's Pharaoh still hanging on to his ego, not able to allow them to do something bigger than him in the world. In fact, when Moshe and Aharon, finish warning Pharaoh about the locusts, it says:

וַיִּפֶן וַיֵּצֵא מֵעִם פַּרְעֹה

Without any dismissal, they turn around and walk out on Pharaoh (10:6). So Pharaoh calls them back in! Why?

וַיְגָרֶשׁ אֹתָם מֵאֵת פְּנֵי פַרְעֹה
"And Pharaoh threw them out." (10:11)

He calls them back into the room, just so he can make a show of throwing them out. Crazy...

In contrast, at this same crossroads in the series of plagues, we see Moshe's way of humble alignment beginning to blossom.

Locusts is the first plague where God does not instruct Moshe with a specific warning to issue to Pharaoh. God tells Moshe to warn Pharaoh about further coming danger, to issue a general warning. Yet, when Moshe comes in he talks specifically about the locusts, even though there's nothing in the Torah that indicates that God told him this.

There are two possible explanations for how Moshe could have made a specific call, without God telling him the Divine plan. Possibility Number One: Moshe actually called this one, and then Hashem fulfilled it. Possibility Number Two: That Moshe was so in tune at this point, that he was able to intuit — he had a natural sense — of what was coming. He was truly, so to speak, "in the zone." He was completely aligned with Hashem's will, and he could see the natural manifesting pattern.

Whichever way we look at it, we are seeing a transformed Moshe, who's gone from being this very reluctant servant without confidence, to becoming a person of high confidence, speaking with clarity of vision.

Compare the Moshe we see now, with the Moshe we saw at the second plague of frogs. Back then, after he warns Pharaoh about the frogs we see Moshe go into a panic! The Torah tells us he went out from Pharaoh and cried out to God: "Oh my God! I told him this plague is coming! It's gotta happen!" He's absolutely frantic.

Yet now we see a Moses who's a real smooth character. He's really in the groove. He's able to call out the plagues without even having clear instruction. He goes and he speaks to Pharaoh, and he walks out without even being given leave.

We see this same contrast of personalities and approaches to life again after the plague of Darkness.

Pharaoh summons Moshe and Aaron, and this is the first time Pharaoh doesn't say "Hashem **your** God," he says:

לְכוּ֙ עִבְד֣וּ אֶת־ה'

"Go ahead and serve God…"

But then again Pharaoh has a condition.

רַ֧ק צֹאנְכֶ֛ם וּבְקַרְכֶ֖ם יֻצָּ֑ג

"But you're going to have to leave your shop and cattle behind" (10:24)

In other words, he's still setting conditions on the service of God. Now he acknowledges that there is a God, but he—Pharaoh—still gets to decide how God will be served. He's still trying to hold on to some semblance of control. He cannot open his imagined grip on the events of life.

But Moshe calls him on it. He says, "What are you talking about? We're going to bring everything with us, because we're there to serve God, with whatever's required to serve God. You don't get to set preconditions."

And Pharaoh gets really mad again, he blows up, and he says:

לֵךְ מֵעָלָי הִשָּׁמֶר לְךָ אַל־תֹּסֶף רְאוֹת פָּנַי כִּי בְּיוֹם רְאֹתְךָ פָנַי תָּמוּת

"Don't come in front of me again. If you come in front of me again you're a dead man!" (10:28)

And Moshe cooly replies to him:

וַיֹּאמֶר מֹשֶׁה כֵּן דִּבַּרְתָּ לֹא־אֹסִף עוֹד רְאוֹת פָּנֶיךָ

"Just like you said. You won't be seeing me again." (10:29)

Wow! What a different Moshe!

This is not a guy who is worried about having a speech impediment, fumbling around for the words. This guy is in the zone! He's not the guy who's walking out and thinking, "Ah you know what I should've said? I know what I should've said…"

Moshe is on the money. He takes Pharaoh's words and he throws them back in his face without blinking, without hesitation. We see such a difference. We see such a transformation of Moshe here.

In contrast, the tragic transformation of Pharaoh comes after the final plague— after the death of the firstborn children (and the firstborn animals). After this final plague, Pharaoh calls to Moshe and we finally see a Pharaoh who is able to release his grip on the illusion of Force and control, and to recognize Hashem and the guiding hand of the Divine.

וַיִּקְרָא לְמֹשֶׁה וּלְאַהֲרֹן לַיְלָה

"He called them that night…"

וַיֹּאמֶר קוּמוּ צְּאוּ מִתּוֹךְ עַמִּי גַּם־אַתֶּם גַּם־בְּנֵי יִשְׂרָאֵל וּלְכוּ עִבְדוּ אֶת־ה
כְּדַבֶּרְכֶם

"Go serve God as you say it should be done, as you've spoken…"

No more limitations, no more control, no more authority, no more posturing.

גַּם־צֹאנְכֶם גַּם־בְּקַרְכֶם קְחוּ כַּאֲשֶׁר דִּבַּרְתֶּם וָלֵכוּ

"…take your sheep and your cattle, take everything just like you said and go…"

And here is the painful, tragic passage that are Pharaoh's last words to Moshe and Aaron:

וּבֵרַכְתֶּם גַּם־אֹתִי

"And please will you also bless me?"

Pharaoh has destroyed everything through his ego, and only in finally confronting the total destruction of everything, does he realize that the source of blessing comes from humble alignment.

One more note on the whole 'God hardening Pharaoh's heart' question…

This whole idea of Pharaoh and free will, and the questions around God's hardening of Pharaoh's heart, is really a very deep matter.

To me it's always been amazing that we have a question about it at all. We're saying, "How could Hashem harden Pharaoh's heart?" What do you mean "How could Hashem?" Hashem can do whatever He wants! What do you mean?

So firstly, it reveals to us something very visceral about our sense of free will and its importance to us. Why does it get us so riled up, this notion, this possibility that God might be taking away someone's free will? It's so upsetting to us!

But Pharaoh is a bad cat, so shouldn't we by happy that he might lose his free will? And yet we are still so upset by it, by just the possibility that God would do such a thing. It's so disturbing. It upsets us on a visceral level.

So of course, we already have a tidy answer, as we already discussed, that God was giving Pharaoh and his servants the ability to *maintain* their free will, because without God's giving them an extra boost of 'heart-toughness' they would have lost their ability to choose whether or not to stand up against God!

Yet this very deep idea brings up another question.

Why would God *let* a person like Pharaoh go toe to toe with Him? Why wouldn't God put the brakes on him?

If someone's going to be that bad and do that much wrong, why doesn't God stop them?

So we hit God from both sides! We say, *'How can you take away a person's free will?!'* And then we say, *'Why doesn't God take away the free will of evil people?! Why doesn't God intervene and do something?!'*

This underscores something so fundamental about our humanity. Our sense of free will is so fundamental to who we are as human beings. It is the essence of the Divine Spark within each of us. It is what gives us our Godly element. And we all have it.

It is what gives life meaning.

If somebody comes to us and tells us what to do, even if it was something we might have wanted to do, the second someone tells us to do it, we don't want to do it anymore!

The difference between a kid and an adult is when someone tells a kid to do something, the kid says no and the kid fights them because *"don't tell me what to do!"*

Hopefully, as grown ups we've learned that sometimes we need to play along and we need to comply. But we don't comply because we want to. The child inside us is still ticked off! We comply because we've reached that point in maturity where we realize that even though we don't want to comply when someone tells us what to do, sometimes it's still in a our best interest to do so. We're smart enough, so to speak, not to cut off our nose to spite our face.

But it doesn't mean we're enjoying it at that point, because we certainly don't. At the end of the day, once someone imposes on, steps on, our free will, we're upset. Very, very upset.

So it's a very deep idea, this riddle in this week's Torah portion, because it connects to the whole idea of Shmirat HaMitzvot, observing the Divine Laws of the Torah. It actually connects to the entire relationship of humanity with God, because the very foundations of creation and the story of the Torah are based upon Hashem giving human beings freedom of choice.

The Torah opens with God offering humanity a world which is literally a Garden of Eden, but offering Adam and Eve the choice: "If you want to do it your own way, according to your own mind, according to your own reasoning, go to that tree, pick a fruit, bite it — and that's your sign that you want to do things your own way." From that point in the Torah it was a downhill run away from HaShem. People always running off toward hedonistic, selfish, egotistical, power, pleasure, and the like. Always running away from Hashem and toward selfish goals.

The first exception to that was Avraham & Sarah, who turned toward Hashem. And throughout the Torah it's always been a story of Hashem waiting for people to choose Him and the Higher Path of Divine ethics.

We were in Mitzrayim, we were slaves in Egypt until exactly the point when we called out to God and asked God to come and get us.

We got the Torah because we wanted it. It wasn't forced on us. (see the meditation of Week 18, Parshat Mishpatim)

We got a Mishkan because we built a golden calf, and even though it was the wrong approach, the fact that we wanted some

kind of a physical structure through which to connect to God —
that request and yearning was honored.

We didn't go into Israel the first time because we didn't want to.
And God waited a full generation of 40 years, until the next
generation complained to Moses and asked "Why are we still
here in the dessert?   Why are we not going forward into the
land?" It was when they chose to go into Israel that they went
there.

The whole Torah is about this one, core theme: Hashem waiting
for people to choose God.

Sometimes I will hear people say, "You know, the problem with
the Torah, the problem with mitzvot, is it's all a bunch of Have
Tos."

I'm always amazed by that, because I know a lot of people who
don't keep the Torah, I know a lot of people who don't keep
Shabbat, I know people who don't keep kosher, I know people
who don't pray, I know people who don't put on tefillin, I know
people who don't light Shabbat candles, I know people who don't
do the mitzvot of the Torah.

I know Christians who don't follow their faith, I know Muslims
who don't follow their faith.

The thing is, all of these people who are not, so to speak, doing
what God told them to do — no one is getting struck by lightning.
No one is being struck down. And so this idea that *we have to*,
that the Torah is just a whole bunch of *Have Tos*, that God is all

about the Have To... God is the least about Have To as any present being in our lives.

People are about Have Tos. Hashem is not.

Hashem has always been waiting for the **Want To**.

And even with a guy like Pharaoh — such a bad cat doing so much harm, so much wrong — God goes out of God's way to make sure that Pharaoh still gets to choose what he wants.

Perhaps the most beautiful part of the entire story is at the end of Parshat Bo, after the striking of the first born, when Pharaoh, rather than voicing anger at God, says, "Please, will you bless me too?"

That's all Hashem has ever been waiting for.

Whether we're a Moshe, or, God forbid, we're a little like a Pharaoh right now, our freedom of choice is in our hands.

God's partnership in this life is not about force.
God's agenda is not about a bunch of Have Tos.

The whole message, the whole purpose, the whole Divine dream of life is for us to get to *Want To*.

What do you choose, today?

Week 16: The Torah Portion of 'Beshalach'

Free-Fall into Enlightenment

This week's Torah portion has one of my favorite lessons, one of my favorite messages. And it's actually a message that repeats itself a few times in the Torah. We see it in the time of Abraham, in the story of Abraham, and we're going to see it highlighted in this week's Torah portion.

We have to remember that the Torah speaks on two levels. There's the level wherein it's recounting the history of the nascent Jewish nation, and there's another level wherein the Torah is highlighting and teaching us specific lessons.

Not every part of our history is written in the Torah. The reason for this omission of major blocks of our history (like the 40 years of wandering) is that the events that are recounted in the Torah are not only historical, but also teach us important, timeless lessons. It is one of those deep life-lessons that we're going to see in this Torah portion, Beshalach.

The question we're going to look at is: When a person wants to transcend, when a person wants to grow past their boundaries, when a person finds themselves facing limitations, bad habits, a sense of "I'm-not-sure-I-can", and they are trying to break forward to reach a higher level of themselves—or even on the deepest level to reach *enlightenment* — the question is: *How do we do that?* How do we achieve and realize that transcending aspiration?

What we have here in the Torah is a very strange story. God has come to liberate the Jewish people. He performs ten miraculous plagues, true suspensions of nature. He leads the Jewish people out of Egypt. He leads them up to an ocean, and there they are encamped by the edge of this ocean. Suddenly, Pharaoh and his entire army come descending upon their fragile camp!

And the Jewish people, quite understandably, are panic-stricken! They call out to Moshe and they say, "What have you done to us?! We told you this would happen! We told you: 'Isn't it better to live as slaves, than to be set free to die in the Wilderness?' And here, look! We're going to die!"

And Moshe confidently says to the Jewish people:

וַיֹּאמֶר מֹשֶׁה אֶל־הָעָם֮ אַל־תִּירָ֒אוּ֒

"Don't be afraid…'"

הִֽתְיַצְּב֗וּ וּרְאוּ֙ אֶת־יְשׁוּעַ֣ת ה' אֲשֶׁר־יַעֲשֶׂ֥ה לָכֶ֖ם הַיּ֑וֹם

"'…wait and see the salvation that God is going to do for you today!" (Exodus 14:13)

And he goes on to say that God will wage war on their behalf. Sounds good!

But God responds to Moshe in a surprising way, and says:

וַיֹּאמֶר ה' אֶל־מֹשֶׁה מַה־תִּצְעַק אֵלָ֑י

"HaShem says to Moshe, 'Why are you screaming out to Me?'"

דַּבֵּר אֶל־בְּנֵי־יִשְׂרָאֵל וְיִסָּעוּ

"Speak to the Jewish people and get going!" (14:15)

Get going?! There's an ocean in front of them! There's an army descending upon them from the only other land-passage! Where exactly are they supposed to go??

And to make things just a little bit stranger, we're told by the great commentator Rashi, later on in the book of Bamidbar ('Numbers', the fourth book of the Torah), that the sea did not split until one particular member of the people—this fellow *Nachshon ben Aminadav*—walked into the ocean up to his nose! Only then did the water split…

So the question is: What is the symbolism and relevance of this hidden story that Rashi reveals to us? What is the significance of the fact that someone had to walk into the ocean "up to his nose" in order for the sea to split? Why did the circumstances require that specific action?

And of course, the deeper question is: What's going on? Why did God set up the Jewish people like this? And why, when Moshe says, "Watch what God's gonna do," does God suddenly say, "Get walking. Get going. Don't even ask me for help!" *Where were they supposed to go?*

So let's break it down…

Concept 1: When we look at that idea of transcendence, the Egyptian people in Hebrew are called the *Mitzrim,* and Egypt is called *Mitzrayim.* Mitzrayim can also be read *Meitzarim* — which in English means 'constraints', 'from the straits', 'from the narrows', 'from the confinement'.

My teacher Rabbi Rachmiel from Ohr Sameach taught me that an exception in the Hebrew language emphasizes this symbolism: In Hebrew, when we refer to a native of a particular land, we always add the phonetic "ee" to the end of the name of that land. So for Israel we say Israeli. And for America we say America'ee. And for France — in Hebrew its Tzarfat — we say Tzarfatee. But for Mitzrayim, Egypt, we don't see Mitzrayimee, which would be proper grammar. Instead we say *Mitzree*. We emphasize the Hebrew root-word *Meitzar* again, this word for the narrows, the straits, the constraints, the restriction, the limitation...

And so symbolically, Biblical Egypt represents a person who is confined by his or her own limitations.

Concept 2: What narrative, in our Parsha, represents that idea of a person trying to break out of their boundaries? What event illustrates a person stuck in his or her habits who wants to break out? What is the *first step in the process of wanting to transcend yourself*, of wanting to break free?

The first step we see is:

וישמע ה׳ את צעקה גדולה ומרה

"God heard their great and anguished cry."

The first thing we need is that *we must <u>want</u> to change*. The first step in changing our reality is *wanting to change*. And not just a little bit. Why does it say God heard the *"great, anguished cry"*, this deep, profound battle cry?

Because it's got to be all or nothing. If a person 99% wants to change, that one percent is going to trip them up...

Transformation — true transformation, true transcendence — is *all or nothing*.

It's *in or out*. There's no neutral anymore. It's *"I gotta get out of here!!!"*

And so the first step is this calling out to God. It's this complete 'calling out from the depths of our soul' and saying, "I want to transform!" Calling out to HaShem and asking HaShem to help us.

Concept 3: The next step in transcendence is God's loving response — God's incredible helping hand when a person is really ready to transcend. And what in our Parsha represents this?

God, performing the Ten Plagues...

When we call out to God, and we really attach ourselves to our commitment, and we have this desire to transform, a desire and yearning that comes from deep within us — God will help us with our first ten, huge steps. The first ten steps of our journey 'into the new' will seem miraculous. We'll just go and go, until we feel like "Wow! Nothing can get in my way!!"

But then comes Concept 4: God takes us and He helps us to transform our inertia from being stagnant and stationary, to getting into movement and motion. But at a certain point, the path we're on — that path of of transcendence towards enlightenment — has to become our own. It has to become clear to us, within ourselves. And the real moment of transformation is when, feeling our momentum — knowing we're in the zone, knowing the time is *NOW* — *we begin to walk on our own*.

Transcendence takes place in *that* moment, when when we finally let go, when we finally free-fall into a new 'me'. We let go of our past, we let go of our old attachments, and we free-fall into the future. *We free-fall into the potential of what we can become.* *That* is the moment of transformation.

This is the moment at the shores of the Red Sea, when God responds to the people and Moses, and says: "Why are you crying out to me? Get up and go on your own!" It's up to you now; either you will let your old habits overtake you again, or you will summon the resolve and absolute conviction from within that the only way *is forward.*

We see this lesson first presented in the story of Avraham. Because the story of Avraham starts out with God saying to Avraham, *"Lech Lecha—go to yourself."* The Hebrew words literally mean "go to yourself." It's a journey to the self. And he says *"mi artzecha, mi moladetecha, mi beit avicha* — from your land, from your birthplace, from your father's home — *el haaretz asher areka* — to the place that I will show you."

Now, those are very weird directions. What kind of directions are these really?

Imagine I'm giving someone directions and I say, "OK, you want to get to my house? Right now you're standing on a corner in

New York. You're right by the Empire State Building. And across from you is a record store."

And you're like, "Yeah?"

And I'm like, "And when you get to my house, it will be my house."

"What? Dude, I need directions. You gotta describe to me *where I'm going, not where I am!* I know where I am."

But the journey of the self, what God is saying to Avraham, is that the journey of the self is about — you have all these things you know, you have all that's familiar to you — but the journey of the self is about letting go of what's familiar, in order to find something that you won't see until you let go of everything that's familiar to you.

There's a great poster that I had when I was a kid, that I gave to my kids, and it hangs on the wall in their room. And it's a poster with a quote from a fellow named Charles Dubois. It says, "The important thing is this: To be able to sacrifice, at any moment, what we are for what we can become."

That's the idea we have here.

So what happens is that when God hears our cry, the cry will be answered. When we want to change, HaShem will help us to change. And HaShem will lead us in the most wondrous ways towards that transformation. He'll take us 10 great steps forward!

But once we have momentum, it's time for us to decide. And at that moment, we either find the strength to go forward, or else the boundaries that were holding us back — the boundaries that we just got free of — will come and pull us back under again, and we'll find ourselves right back where we started.

> There's a story I once heard about a man who had a crisis of faith. He went to his Rabbi and told him that he was losing his faith in God and the Mitzvot (the life-guiding principles) of the Torah. When his Rabbi asked him "Why", the man explained:
>
> "A few months ago I started praying the morning prayers, every morning, for the first time in my life. And Rabbi, it was crazy! Everything started going amazingly in my life! My business! My personal life! Everything just started clicking.
>
> But then suddenly, after months of this, a few weeks ago a very important deal in my business fell through. And last week I got into a terrible fight with my girlfriend. You see Rabbi, I thought the daily prayers were really helping me, but now I see that they don't do anything at all. And this is my crisis of faith!
>
> What is happening, Rabbi? Why has God stopped listening to my prayers?"
>
> And that Rabbi looked at the man, and gently said: "My sweetest friend, I assure you that God is still listening to your prayers. The only thing that has changed, is that God has stopped bribing you to pray each day!"

When we are ready to grow, ready to transcend, God will lead us through the first ten huge steps. But at a certain moment it has to become our own. At a certain point, we must come to know the path for ourselves.

And now, Concept 5: What was the significance of what Nachshon did, that his action had the power to split the sea? Why did Nachson have to walk in up to his nose? Why is this so important for Rashi to emphasize? And why has this seemingly anecdotal story become so well-known in today's Jewish world?

Because if you walk into an ocean up to your chin, you can still breathe.
And if you walk in up to your mouth, you can still breathe.
But when you walk in up to your nose, *you can't breathe anymore*.
That is the moment of Truth. That is the moment of commitment.
That is the trust-fall into a new future — a new YOU.

The Jewish people knew. They knew which way was forward. They knew which way they needed to go. And for Nachshon, as a representative of his newborn Nation, there was no ocean in front of them. There was no boundary. There were no more limitations! There was the pure opportunity to transcend, to transform, and to grow forward into the next clear and powerful step.

The thing is, when a person can achieve that,
when a person can trust-fall into their moment of potential,
when they let go and realize that the momentum is within them,
and that HaShem is with them and *that the time is now*,

and they realize that there are no more obstacles anymore,
then the obstacles in fact melt away before them.
That's when we really transcend.

Finally, the other side of of this Moment of Transcendence is Concept 6: The receiving of the Torah. The receiving of the Torah represents sustained transcendence, *the Sustainable High.* *It represents Enlightenment.*

So let's go back to that lazy moment in our Torah portion, when we are standing there by the edge of the Sea and God says: "It's not about calling out to me to hold your hand anymore. It's not about me fighting your battles for you anymore. Yes, I will always help you break free! Yes, I will always help you find your momentum! Yes, I will always help set you on the path…"

But the real moment of enlightenment is not about what HaShem can do for us. Rather, it's when we reach the level where it's not about calling out to God to pave the way for us anymore.
It's when we reach the level of Avraham, the level of "Lech Lecha."
Of discovering the Divine potential for transformation within each and every one of us.
Of letting go of that which is familiar, to free-fall into the opportunity of that which we can become.

When we do that, even oceans will melt away before us, and transcendence and enlightenment will await us on the other side.

Week 17: The Torah Portion of 'Yitro'

A Choice for Everyone

It's kind of interesting… In this week's Torah portion, Yitro, we find the Jewish people about to receive the Torah. And right before receiving the Torah, God tells Moses, "I need you to give the Jewish people a message." And that message is one which, to say the least, might be a bit controversial for some.

God says, "Tell the Jewish people the following:"

אַתֶּם רְאִיתֶם אֲשֶׁר עָשִׂיתִי לְמִצְרָיִם וָאֶשָּׂא אֶתְכֶם עַל־כַּנְפֵי נְשָׁרִים וָאָבִא אֶתְכֶם אֵלָי

"You saw what I did in Egypt, when I lifted you on the wings of eagles and brought you close me…"

וְעַתָּה אִם־שָׁמוֹעַ תִּשְׁמְעוּ בְּקֹלִי וּשְׁמַרְתֶּם אֶת־בְּרִיתִי וִהְיִיתֶם לִי סְגֻלָּה מִכָּל־הָעַמִּים כִּי־לִי כָּל־הָאָרֶץ

"And now, if you will listen to my voice and if you will keep my covenant, then you will be a treasure to me among all the nations, for all the world is mine…"

וְאַתֶּם תִּהְיוּ־לִי מַמְלֶכֶת כֹּהֲנִים וְגוֹי קָדוֹשׁ

"And you will become my kingdom of priests and sacred nation…" (Exodus 19:4-6)

And so here we have it, the famous idea of Jewish chosenness. And a lot of people — understandably so — feel upset and offended by this idea. And I'm not talking only about non-Jewish people, although that's also true. I'm talking about sensitive Jewish people, too. Because certainly, we ourselves have suffered enough persecution over the centuries by other people who have thought that they were more 'chosen' than we are. And very often we suffered that prejudice under persecution, pogroms and genocide. So how do we, as a people who have endured the horrors of such attitudes, turn around and espouse the very views under which we suffered such nightmarish persecution?

Is it one and the same?
Or is there something different here?
Is there something distinct which we can come to understand and learn from?

Over the past many years, a number of rabbis and Jewish leaders have been invited to come sit with the Dali Lama. The Dali Lama seeks to learn from them ideas of how his people — Tibetan Buddhists — can manage to survive in their exile, in their diaspora. And the Dali Lama believes that he can learn this from the Jewish people specifically.

Now of course, one of the questions that these rabbis asked of the Dali Lama was: 'Why us? After all, it doesn't help if I take a lesson on how to preserve oranges from the way that I grow tulips. If it's a different species, so to speak, a different kind of reality, then what relevance do the lessons have?' So they asked him: 'Why do you think that we have something in common?'

And without missing a beat, the Dali Lama replied, and I quote: "I think we are both chosen people. We do not have exactly the same idea, but we Tibetans believe we were chosen by Avalokitesvara, the embodiment of Buddha's compassion, the protector deity of Tibet. You believe you were chosen by the Creator God. So it is almost the same idea. Another reason: When we became refugees, we knew that our struggle would not be easy, it would take a long time — generations. Very often, we reference to history of the Jewish people, of how they kept their identity and faith despite such hardship and so much suffering. And how, when the conditions were ripe, they were ready to rise again and rebuild their nation. So you see, there are many things to learn from our Jewish brothers and sisters."

Amazing…

Now, what's especially interesting about this is, (and I don't know if the Dali Lama knew this or not, and how schooled he is regarding the subtleties of the Torah text), but what's especially interesting about his reply to the rabbis is that *he's quite right to compare our chosenness.* He's quite right on a deeper level, because there are two other significant traditions of Buddhism that are shared with Judaism, and both are quite relevant to how we both think about the concept of 'being chosen'.

The first is that they don't proselytize, and the second is that they are open to everybody. And while the second idea of being open to everyone might not immediately draw an association with Judaism for many people, that is only because of how far we have strayed from our course during our long exile.

In the times of our Temples, we graciously accepted and offered sacrifices brought by non-Jewish kingdoms from around the world. And our scholars and sages were well-known for their interactions and friendships with leaders of other faiths.

These two principles help us frame a very deep idea that enables us to understand the difference between the Jewish/Buddhist concept of chosenness, versus that of the Nazis and driven-by-force Movements like the Crusaders. There is a vast chasm of difference between a claim of chosenness which is exclusive, and thereby breeds bigotry, racism, hatred and genocide throughout generations, in contrast to a vision of chosenness which is *inclusive*, and which is about *raising banners of light and goodness* in order to *share and illuminate the world around us,* so that every person and nation in the world can find their own path.

So let's take a look at the Torah again, and let's go back to some earlier parts of the Torah and consider a couple of quick things.

Why does the Torah start with Adam and Eve, and then with Noah and his family? If the Torah is just about the Jewish people and about our private club, well let's just talk about the Jewish people and our private club! These two stories have nothing to do with us!

But they do. Because they serve as an important message from God to us, saying, "What do I want when I create a world? I'll tell you..."

If Adam and Eve would have walked in God's ways, who would have been God's 'chosen people'? And the answer of course, is: *Everybody*. And again, when God reboots the world, if Noah and his family would have walked in God's ways, who would have been God's chosen people? The answer, again, is: *Everyone*.

So what went wrong? The answer is simply that in any meaningful relationship, it's not a meaningful relationship if the other side is coerced. In order for God to have a meaningful relationship with humanity, people need to have free will. God therefore chose to give us the gift of free will, and with that gift we have the choice to accept a relationship with Him, or turn away from it. Very sadly, humanity, since the very beginning of time until today, has consistently turned away from God and run after things like hedonism, property and power.

Ten generations after Noah, in a world that kept going on a downhill run away from God, two people got up and started walking the other way: Avraham and Sarah. These two people decided that there was a greater reason to live, that there was a greater purpose to life. They believed in a higher morality, and while everyone around them was running downhill away from godliness, they turned around and started climbing back up that hill, back up against all odds.

When we put these early parts of the Torah together, we begin to get a more complete understanding of the Jewish concept of chosenness. Firstly, it's important to realize where the choice starts. With the stories of Adam & Eve and Noah, God made it clear: God chooses everyone. But Got was waiting for humanity to choose Him in return. With Avraham and Sarah, God found that first reciprocation by humanity.

It is in this spirit that God said to Avraham (in the opening of the Torah portion of Lech Lecha): "In choosing Me, there's a blessing for you. Because what I desire in My world is that goodness begets goodness, righteousness begets righteousness. Choosing to live a moral, ethical life and choosing to pursue goodness and lovingkindness and to connect to godliness in life — it will produce its own rewards. And yes, that means that you will survive and there will be blessing in your generations like nobody's ever seen!"

But then God explains the intent of this special blessing with it's conclusion, when God says:

וְנִבְרְכוּ בְךָ כָּל מִשְׁפְּחֹת הָאֲדָמָה

The first time we meet Avraham and Sarah, God says,

> *"And you will bring the blessing back <u>to all the families of the world</u>" (Genesis, 12:3).*

The message is clear: "<u>I'm not looking for a private club</u>. *I'm looking to see all of My children come home.*

How will they come home? Because your righteous way of living will produce such amazing results for you and your generations, that people will take notice and they will see the rewards and blessings that *alignment* and a life of goodness yields."

"And in turn, the blessing of that relationship with Me" — and God calls it *a blessing* — "will reach everybody on earth one day."

That's God's wish.
That's God's dream.
It was God's dream in creating the world,
and it's God's dream when He speaks to Avraham.

When God later speaks to Yitzchak and Yaakov (Isaac & Jacob), He repeats to them similarly, but not exactly the same:

וְנִבְרְכוּ בְךָ כָּל העמים

> *"And through you the blessing will reach to all the nations…"*

It's not about *converting* nations.

It's not *"go out and make one nation."*

It's not "go out and proselytize."

Rather, it's about extending the canopy of blessing, through example, to include everyone. By choice.

The message is simple: *'Live righteously. The results, for you and your generations, will be evident to all. And when other nations and peoples see the blessing that comes from choosing a loving relationship with Me and living a noble life, they will reach for the same blessing. And yes, I'm waiting for them. The blessing is there for them to enjoy, too. Each nation and peoplehood in their own way.'*

Over the years I have found that this idea of Inclusive Chosenness really surprises most people. But when we look at it, it really shouldn't.

I'm blessed to have spent fifteen years leading an organization that helped thousands of young teens get through tough times and make positive life-choices. One of the messages that I shared with these kids all the time is that *each one of them matters*. There's no redundancy among humanity. No two people are the same. No two human beings are here in the world for the same reason. We each have a purpose, and each one is unique. We each have something special and essential to bring to the world.

And it's that sense of specialness — that sense of uniqueness — that calls us to carry forward to find our song, and to bring our song into the harmony of life. Because if we think about it for a second, we can readily see how important a harmony of individual and unique people is to the symphony of humanity. Would we really want a world where everybody was the same? Would we really want a world where every flower smelled the same? Where all trees looked alike? Where all animals looked alike?

If we think about it for a moment, we see the importance, *we see the splendor* that shines from each individual human being and every unique society, just like flowers and trees, and the birds and their songs. We can readily see that everyone is precious, and that True Harmony comes from all of those different instruments and notes being woven together into a symphony. It's not about one voice, but rather about reaching a harmony of different voices singing together — not in conflicting keys, but together — an orchestra of unique and complimentary instruments.

And this is why the Jewish people do not proselytize, but instead joyously share our ideals and our values with the world around us.

Returning to our Torah portion, *this is the idea* that God is sharing with the young Jewish Nation that is now being born.

First of all, we have to understand the premise: Like Avraham, they made a choice, and God was right there waiting. Waiting to be chosen by humanity. God is always waiting. When we call, God is always right there. The Jews were living in Egypt for hundreds of years. What started up this renewed relationship of

Avraham's descendants with God? It was when the people called out to God! God said to Moses, "I heard their cry…"

And so we called out to God, and God answered us. And that is why HaShem says: "When you reach out to me for a True Relationship, I will lift you on the wings of eagles." Because there are no limitations on human potential. *When we reach out the right way, when we reach out in justice and righteousness and kindness and love, we climb upon the wings of eagles. Nothing is impossible.*

And in the next phrase God says: "Now, if you will listen to my voice and keep my covenant…"
What covenant?
The covenant God made with Avraham, Yitzchak and Yaakov.
What covenant was that?
A covenant about a blessing for the sake of *sharing a blessing*.
An inclusive blessing.
Not an exclusive blessing.

"I will be with you, if you will keep my ways…"

The blessing of God is contingent upon our living a certain way — the blessings are a result of the choices we make. The blessings are the natural result of righteous choices yielding inspiring results. In such a scenario, then yes, the Jewish Nation will be a treasure to HaShem among all the nations.

Now, consider the state of the other Nations of the world at that time. We're dealing with a world of violent idolators, who engage in human sacrifice! We're dealing with a world where people were sacrificing their very children to inanimate objects! So yes, it's going to be a pretty glaring difference. And despite this, God says, "It's not about proselytizing. Be patient. People will notice that goodness begets goodness. That is the treasure of walking with Me. Give it time…"

In bestowing this blessing upon the Jewish people, God says very importantly, "You'll be a nation of **priests**." And that word is *very important.*

Because the thing about the Kohen (the priest) among the Jewish people, is that they had no portion in the land of Israel. And what does that mean?   It means this: The only way the Kohen got to eat, is if the Kohen helped the people under his responsibility to connect with God (by helping us bring our offerings — *by service, and not power*). As long as the Kohen helped us connect with God, the Kohen got the first cuts of meat, the first fruits, all the best of the best, like a king!! But if the Kohen wasn't helping the people connect to HaShem, then the Kohen was going hungry…

This is God's message when he tells the Jewish people that "you'll be a nation of priests." Our job is to be "a light unto the nations." Our job is to lift this banner, to set an example: The blessings of HaShem — through the practices of Spiritual Harmony — can ultimately be something that's enjoyed by all peoples of the world, each according to their own path.

HaShem says, "If you serve humanity this way, as priests in the service of creating and sharing connection with Me, you'll get the best of the best! You'll have a beautiful land and enjoy extraordinary blessing! You'll beat back the Romans! You'll beat back the Ancient Egyptians! You'll beat back the Greeks! It'll be amazing. You'll survive throughout all of world history!

But if you forget to lift that banner,

if you forget to set that example,

if you forget that message of inclusiveness and social responsibility,

then you are going to go hungry.

You'll lose the land.

And you'll spend 2,000 years homeless in exile, simply struggling to survive…"

It is not by accident that we conclude the Yom Kippur prayer of Musaf every year, that holy sacred prayer, with the following passage from Isaiah:

עוֹלֹתֵיהֶם וְזִבְחֵיהֶם לְרָצוֹן עַל מִזְבְּחִי כִּי בֵיתִי בֵּית תְּפִלָּה יִקָּרֵא לְכָל הָעַמִּים

*"One day your offerings will find favor before Me, when My house is called a house of God **by all the nations of the world**." (Isaiah, 56:7)*

It's not about *one nation*. It's not about the Jewish nation.

It's about every nation.

Because every person matters to HaShem.

May we all be blessed to discover our individual songs, and to experience the joy of seeing the goodness that comes from positive choices. And may each of us lift a banner that inspires those around us to live more righteous and meaningful lives.

We are each already chosen.   HaShem is just waiting for us to 'choose Him', too.

Week 18: The Torah Portion of 'Mishpatim'

Wow, Does God Believe in You!

This whole Torah thing is a little bit difficult.

And not just the whole Torah thing—the whole God thing.

It's just too much, and a little bit overwhelming. Because seriously, we're only human. How are we supposed to satisfy God?

I've been talking a lot with different people over the past week and the conversation's come up again and again, which is not a new conversation for me, but it's interesting how much it's come up over the past week. This idea of God, and the fact that in our modern vernacular, God has really become a little bit of a nasty word, if you will.   And I stress the expression "nasty _word_" because it really is the _word_ "God" that we don't like.

What do I mean by that?

Sometimes I do these workshops with teens, and a question I ask them is: Who here believes in God? And most of the time, a good group of hands will go up from people who do believe in God, and also a significant portion of hands will go up from people who do not believe in God.   And I ask those on each side to take a minute to explain to us why they either do or do not believe in God.   I don't challenge their answers.   I just allow the different points of view to be shared, and allow everyone to hear each others' points of view about why they do or do not believe in God.

And then, after all the hands go down and we've talked about this, I ask another question: _Who here believes in Godliness?_

And everyone looks at me kind of strange and, of course, somebody asks: Well, what do you mean by that?

And I explain: *Godliness* is that feeling that we experience when we see a breathtaking rainbow over a field. Or when we stand upon a beach gazing at the sunset, and it's so overwhelmingly beautiful that we look up and down the shore just to see if there's *someone else* on the beach who's seeing the same sunset that we're seeing. Because even though we might not know who they are or even be able to fully see them, just knowing that someone is there sharing in this incredible experience has suddenly become very important to us.

It's when there's a thunderstorm outside and we go out on our porch so that we can *really feel* the thunderstorm and experience that *certain something* stirring inside of us. That *something* that you can never quite describe, but which is really at the core of your very being.

It's the feeling we have when we experience love, when we stare into a beautiful flower or hear a child's laughter.

It's that feeling that somehow deep inside we all know that life is deeper than all of the daily humdrum and ups and downs. That there is something going on that's deeper than anything we ever really talk about. That somehow we are all here for a purpose, and somehow all of this matters on a more profound level than we ever quite put into words.

It's the feeling that ultimately we're all really connected…

And the amazing thing about this follow-up question and explanation, is that invariably every time I have _ever_ discussed it — and I've discussed it in all kinds of classrooms with hundreds of teens from all kinds of backgrounds — eventually everyone agrees that they *know* exactly what I'm talking about! It's not just that they believe in that kind of Godliness, that kind of 'Wow', that kind of awe; but rather, they *know* it. It's innate to them. It's something they know in their most visceral being.

Each and every time I have led one of these workshops, we have always achieved unanimous consensus regarding our knowledge of and connection to Godliness.

And so then I ask the very important question:

> *Who was it, during your life-journey, that you allowed to steal your awareness of, and your intuitive relationship with God — and replace it with their ugly, unpleasant definition of the word "God"?*

Because here's the thing:
That feeling.
That wonder.
That awe.
That wow.
That wonderful feeling…

We all know that.
We all love that.
In fact, we all want more of that in our lives.

Because *that—that feeling*—it's wonderful!   It's perfect.   It's Awesome...

But the problem is that this word "God", in the popular vernacular, has become associated with such painful, negative imagery. The emotions and feelings conjured up by hearing the word "God" seem to invoke this figure who's a bully, who's pretty angry most of the time, and who is often — if not always — disappointed with us. Most of the time, we imagine He just wants to kick our butt, because obviously we're doing something wrong and causing him some kind of great displeasure with our constant mistakes and misbehavior.

So, **NO.** We don't like that God. We don't like that word. Because that word and its definition: *BLEAH!!*   Who **would** like it?

The pain that it comes from, how It evolved, well, that's its own discussion. But the fact is, the reason we don't like it, is because *it doesn't match with what we feel on the inside*. It doesn't match — even more deeply — with what we *know* on the inside.

And the thing is, that thing which we each know on the inside — deep, deep inside — *we all want more of it*.

Rabbi Shlomo Carlebach, may his memory be a blessing, used to always teach: "It's so important that rather than telling our children how much they should believe in God, we need to teach our children how much *God believes in them*."

Because you see, that's the point. We're here! We're alive! *Don't you see how much God believes in you??*

It's not about God *demanding something* of us.
It's about God *rooting for us,* and wishing for us that we will experience the highest potential of each moment!
It's about God wanting us to experience the deepest joy, and literally dance with Him throughout the day, every day, *knowing that He is in our corner cheering for us!*
It's about God even tipping the scales in our favor, because guess what? *God wants us to win.* He wants us to succeed! He wants us *to enjoy...*

This idea comes out in this week's Torah portion of Mishpatim. On the surface, this Torah portion seems to be quite overwhelming. It's got so many discussions about so many ideas. It's just nonstop. We get this break down of a whole bunch of directives that just goes on and on and on...

It talks about the slaves, the maidservants. It talks about manslaughter and murder. It talks about injury and repair, and it talks about kidnapping. It talks about personal injury. It talks about personal damages. It talks about animals that kill people. It talks about negligence with property. It talks about stealing. It talks about damage by fire. It talks about people who are responsible for watching the property of others. It talks about borrowed items. It talks about seduction. It talks about lending money, the issue of interest, and being compassionate to poor people. It talks about accepting authority and about justice.

It goes through all of these different discussions, and it gets a little bit overwhelming.

But the thing is that all of this leads up to an amazing phrase, and in that phrase we understand something so deep about the nature of our relationship with God. Through that phrase we understand how things are really meant to be and what it's all really about. Because you see, this expression comes at the conclusion of this section about all the laws, and we're told that it's *through this expression* that we merit the receiving of the Torah.

Our choice of these words is the reason why God chose to bestow His Torah — the very blueprint of Creation, the keys to unlocking all of the wonders of the world — upon His Nation of Israel.

The Torah tells us that Moses took this Book of the Covenant that he was writing, and he read from it in front of all the people. And the people said:

נַעֲשֶׂה וְנִשְׁמָע

"We will do, and we will hear." (Exodus 24:7)

So wait: It's because of that phrase—"we will do, and we will hear"—that we merited to receive the Torah?
Not because of everything that happened until then?
Not because of our following God out into the Wilderness?
Not because of the faith we maintained through all of those hundreds of years of bondage?
Not because since the Exodus we were keeping the Shabbat and we were gathering the Manna in perfect faith?

Not because of any of these things???
Not even because of what took place during the Utterances of the Ten Commandments before the receiving of the Torah??

Nope! We are told that the Jewish Nation merited to receive the Torah because of this phrase: *"We will do, and we will hear."*

To emphasize this point, there is actually an ancient traditional story that's told, a *Midrash*, that tells of God actually going around to the other nations of the world, and asking each nation, "Do you want my Torah?"

And each nation replied, "Well, what's in this Torah?"

And He would tell them what was in it, and then, for one reason or another they would say, "No, I'm sorry. That doesn't suit us."

Finally, God came to the Children of Israel and He said, "Do you want my Torah?"

And they said, *"We will do, and we will hear."* They said, "Yes, we do. Now, tell us about what's inside of it...". And in the merit of this unconditional reply, the Children of Israel merited to receive the Torah.

Now, let's think about this story...

Maybe as a kid, when you hear a story like this you're like, "Oh wow, what a beautiful story about faith in God!" But as you get a little bit older you realize there's something wrong with this story that they like to tell us in Sunday school or in yeshiva. Because what are we really saying?

What we seem to be saying is that God chose to give this great gift of His Torah and His wisdom, the very keys to the universe, to a group of people because *they were consumer suckers*. I mean, let's face it. Who buys a car without looking under the hood?!

Imagine this: Imagine I came up to you and I said, "Hey, do you want to buy a...?"
And before I can even finish my sentence, you exclaim, "Yes!"
"Yes what?"
"Yes, I want to buy it!"
"I didn't even tell you what *it* was."
"That's OK."
"Alright! DEAL!!"

It's simply ridiculous. Seriously. What is that? God chose to gives us His Torah because we were consumer suckers who were willing to buy anything without even knowing what we're getting into?! Wow. How very inspiring...

So what is it then? Why was this phrase so meritorious?

And the answer is: This phrase— נַעֲשֶׂה וְנִשְׁמָע "we will do, and we will hear"—it's not just a phrase in the Torah. Amazingly, it is an expression that first shows up in our 3,500-year-old text, and is an expression that we still use today in modern language!

When somebody you love and who loves you deeply — a parent, a spouse, a sibling, a best friend, a boyfriend, a girlfriend —

comes up to you and says, "Hey, can you do me a favor?" What's your answer?

Your answer is: "Sure. What is it?"

That's a modern way of saying: וְנַעֲשֶׂה וְנִשְׁמָע! That's: "I'll do it. Now, let me hear it."

But when a stranger comes up to you on the street and says, "Hey buddy, can you do me a favor?" What do you say?

Well, you look at them and you say, "It depends. What is it?" ...נִשְׁמָע וְנַעֲשֶׂה.

So what's the difference? Why is it that with someone we love, we say, "Sure, what is it?" And to a stranger we say, "It depends. What is it?" (The latter being, of course, "Let me hear it, and then I'll decide if I'll do it.")

And the answer is that the phrase נַעֲשֶׂה וְנִשְׁמָע, "We will hear, and we will do" — or, "Sure! What is it?" — conveys two important underlying meanings, two important values.

Firstly, the expression conveys *complete trust*. '*I trust you that you would never ask anything of me that would be bad for me. I trust you 100 percent that anything you ask of me is OK for me, and in fact is good for me. I'll jump in head-first, because I trust you.*' It conveys total trust — that I don't need to protect myself from what you might ask of me.

Secondly, it conveys *total commitment*. *'I'm 100 percent committed. I'm 100 percent committed to you. Whatever you ask of me, I **want** to do. I want to do anything I can for you.'* That's love. That's devotion. That's friendship.

And so with somebody whom we love, we say, *"Sure, what is it?"* Because I trust them 100 percent, and I want to give to the them 100 percent. *There's nothing in reserve*. I don't need to protect myself and there's nothing that I *could* give them that I'd want to hold back from them.

Whereas with a stranger, I *don't* trust them. They don't know me enough that I would trust them not to put me at risk. And I don't necessarily want to give them *everything*. That's the difference.

But here's where it gets really interesting. The first thing is this: What God was looking for in humanity was a *relationship with humanity* where we as human beings *trust HaShem*. That we trust God. That God is not out to get us. God is not the boogeyman. God is not the meany in the corner waiting to kick our butt. And this is what our response of *"We will do, and we will hear"* conveyed.

God is our friend. God loves us. God is *all about us*.

I don't need to protect myself from God. I want to give God everything I can. Look how much in my life God has given me! I'm here. I'm breathing. Look at the flowers! Look at the day! Even though you might at times feel that your life is not in order, take a moment and look outside. *Really look outside*. Look at the rhythms. Look at the seasons. Look at the colors. Look at the lines in the bark of a tree. Look at a flower. Watch a bird fly and hear it chirping…

And ask yourself: Is it God who creates disorder in the world? Or is it me? Is it humankind?

Take a moment to realize: I'm part of this world, and I'm here today, and everything is still possible for me…

The Lubavitcher Rebbe, may his memory be a blessing, used to always say: *"Think good; It will be good."*

So נַעֲשֶׂה וְנִשְׁמָע — "We will do, and we will hear" — says: *"I trust God. I want to give everything. There's nothing I'm holding back, and I know there's nothing God would ask of me that wouldn't be good for me. Everything God would ask from me is not because God needs something — because obviously God doesn't need anything. It's because God wants what's best for me!"*

But Wait. Here's where it gets really neat:

If someone you love asks you to do something and for some reason, either practical or emotional, you can't, does that mean your reply of *"Sure, what is it?"* was insincere? Let's say they ask you to take a ladder and get something off of the roof for them, but you're afraid of heights. So you say, "I'd love to but I'm actually petrified of heights. I'm afraid that I'll fall just from the vertigo!" Does that mean that when you said "Sure" you were disingenuous? Does that mean that the statement of love and trust and commitment wasn't sincere?

Of course not!

And let's say that they elaborate after you said *"Sure, what is it?"*, and it turns out they need you on Tuesday. But Tuesday you are going to be out of town! Physically, it's not possible for you to do it. Does that mean that your 100% commitment to them was disingenuous?

Of course not!

And so here you see *the most important point of all*:

> There is no hypocrisy, there is no contradiction, between your practical ability to do something — be it due to emotional limitations or physical limitations — and your trust and your love and your commitment to the person across from you!

So too in our relationship with HaShem: There's nothing wrong with my saying, *"I want to do the whole Torah. I am committed to the entire Torah. There's nothing in the Torah — there's nothing that God puts out there — that I don't want to fulfill. I want to do it all. I trust that it's all good...   But I might not be there yet."*

When we think about our connection with HaShem like a relationship, *which is what it is*, which is what *it's all about*, and when we think about our connection to our innate sense of Godliness and all that is most real in the world, then we discover that we **know** something. And that is that *no relationship can* *sustain itself if I feel the need to be false, or to constantly act differently than I feel capable of, or ready for, on the inside.*

Is it OK to sometimes step out of my comfort zone, to reach higher, to go push the limits on a limited basis? Of course!

But that is not a way to *live. It is not a lifestyle.* Because if you live like that in every way, every day, then you're living a lie. And living a lie is not a real relationship anymore. In fact, living a lie *is not being alive.* Living a lie is really being dead. And that's not why HaShem gave us life.

This is the message of our Parsha, our Torah Portion. You've got all these laws, but the 'punchline' that the Torah wants you to know is: נַעֲשֶׂה וְנִשְׁמָע — "We will do, and we will hear." This isn't about God asking of you what you're not able to do. This is about God looking for an authentic relationship with each and every one of us — a relationship of 100% trust and commitment — and a relationship that allows us to grow forward *from where we are.*

_____

Imagine this: You are meeting the greatest, most saintly person in the world today, the greatest Tzadik, the greatest Tzadeket, the most righteous man or woman in the world, and you ask: *"Are you doing it all? Are you doing it all?"*

What would he or she say?

We all know what he or she would say. We all know.

"Not even close..."

And then we would ask: "Well then, what are you doing?"

And he or she would look at you and say, "Well, I'm working on the step in front of me right now."

And then you'd step back and respond, "Wow, that's so cool! Me too. Me too..."

It's OK to accept everything that someone wishes for me, when I know that no one is expecting me to be more than I am right now.

נַעֲשֶׂה וְנִשְׁמָע — "I trust you, God. I want to do whatever I can. There's nothing I'm holding back.

But even though there's nothing holding me back, that doesn't mean that I'm ready for everything at this moment."

And in fact, by the very nature that our Torah and my relationship with God is the relationship of a finite human being with The Infinite Source, by definition I'll never be doing "it all".

But what I'll always be doing is as much as I really can at this moment. I'll always be giving it my all. As I do in every relationship that is built upon love and choice and connection.

I will act with the peace of mind that my heart and soul are fully present and always will be, even if my emotional or physical limitations have not yet caught up with the depth of my love and devotion — whether to my spouse, my friends, my children, my parents, *myself*, or even HaShem.

I can allow myself to be totally devoted, and to let myself jump into that pool of the Godly world I live in, and to connect with everything I *know* and love to be real, because I *know* that there's nothing to be afraid of. I *know* that there's no God to fear. And I know that the not-nice word called "God" that somebody else defined for me — that's not real.

The God I know is 100 percent in my corner.

The God I know believes in me.

And when I know that, I now have the ability to open up my heart and to believe in Him. And even more deeply, to believe in my relationship with Him, and trust in the love that infuses the guidance He has given us.

Week 19: The Torah Portion of 'Teruma'

Learning to Sing in the Choir

This week's Torah portion takes place when Moses has already ascended the mountain, and he is standing before God. God begins to give him instructions on the building of the Tabernacle, which is called 'The Mishkan'. This is very significant, because it would be fair to say that the Mishkan was the first 'House of God' ever built in the world, and was therefore a precursor to the building of synagogues, which in turn was a precursor to building churches, which in turn was a precursor to building mosques. This is the first time that we have the concept of a monotheistic sacred house of worship to commune with an unseeable, infinite God, wherein human beings will enter in order to connect with God and with the Infinite.

And so we have this very, very beautiful idea being presented, with God instructing the building of the Mishkan. There are two interesting ideas that I want to single out, which really, at first glance, seem to conflict with one another.

In the beginning, it's very beautiful how God says to Moses, "Speak to the Children of Israel, and bring to me an offering, from each person according to what their heart tells them. Thus you should bring this offering." (Shemot, 25:2) And a few passages later, God says, "You will make for Me a Temple, and I will dwell in them." (25:8)

Now, the Torah Commentaries jump right away to point out that it should say "Make a Temple, and I will dwell in *it*" (singular). Or it should say "Make Me **many Temples**, many Holy Sanctuaries, and I will dwell in **them**." But HaShem says, "Make Me a Temple, and I will dwell in **them**."

The most common explanation of what HaShem is saying is that *"them"* refers to *"the members of the community that build this Sacred Space for me."* *"When you make this Holy Sanctuary for me, I will dwell within each and every human being in your community."*

This is such a profound and deep idea, and it ties in with the way God said to bring the offerings to build the Mishkan. You will notice God didn't say, "I want each person to bring this specific item or that specific item." Rather, HaShem says that the offerings should come "from each person according to what their heart tells them."

What HaShem is saying is that in order to create this Holy, Sacred place of Spiritual communion between the Divine and human beings, it must be built upon each person bringing what they have in their heart. It must be based upon every person discovering what they have in their heart, and bringing that out into the world.

Ultimately, a Sacred House of Worship is *not about* worshiping God. Because we have to always remember: God is God. God is whole. God is complete. God is perfect. *God isn't missing anything.* God does not *need* anything.

We have to remember that, because often we think that when we pray we're doing something for God. But if that were true, then that would imply that God *needs* something. But God doesn't need anything. Prayer does not do anything *practical* for God.

However, HaShem *does want something* **for us.** Just like a loving parent desires good things for his or her child.

Who benefits from prayer? The answer is: Prayer is doing *something for us*.

What is it doing for me? The answer is: It's helping me to *align myself with the Source*. It's helping me to examine myself, and to go through meditations that allow me to find my place within the greater flow of life.

True Prayer enables me to find my place within the context of everything that's happening around me. It's a time to reflect...

The key, and this is what HaShem is telling us here, is that to enter a Temple, to enter a synagogue or *any* Holy House of Worship, is not about doing God a favor; rather, it is about giving *ourselves* an opportunity to find that Spiritual Spark — that God-Spark, if you will — within *each and every one of us*.

Yet the Torah portion then puzzles us. Because right after presenting us with such a revolutionary idea, about our universal potential as human beings to become vessels of HaShem's Light, the Torah portion turns around and starts assigning limitations!

If the idea, ultimately, is to discover and illuminate this Divine Spark within each and every one of us, and the idea is about the omnipresence of God and the presence of God in all things, then it's very confusing what HaShem does next!

HaShem instructs Moshe regarding the building of the Divine Ark and an inner-sanctum of the Mishkan called the 'Holy of Holies'.

God instructs Moshe to build sacred, exclusive objects and spaces where God's most revealed presence will rest; spaces that only a handful of people (Moshe and the High Priests) will ever use or have access to throughout history! It is from this exclusive Sacred Space that God says he will advise Moshe and the High Priests: *"In this manner I'll give you instructions."* (25:22)

So on the one hand we have this idea of God saying: Come into the Temple. Find the spark. I'm going to dwell in each and every one of you. Which is the idea of saying: It's not that God is *in the Temple*, but really that within the Temple we find that God is *within each and every one of us*.

But then HaShem turns around and is very much limiting His presence and saying to Moshe: I'm going to speak to you from this *very specific, exclusive place*. And until now, don't forget, prophecy happened all over the place! With Abraham and Sarah, and Isaac and Rebecca, and with Jacob and Rachel and Leah, prophecy took place wherever they were! And also for Moshe — The Burning Bush — he was just out there shepherding in the middle of a field in the middle Midian (which was a very idolatrous part of the world), and all of a sudden there's God! And we see God constantly communing with Moshe and Aharon in the land of Egypt!

So it seems almost a contradiction. On the one hand, God is suddenly limiting His presence to such a finite physical place through which to commune. And on the other hand, He's telling us that we're meant to ultimately find this Spark from Him within each and every one of us — every one in their own way and in their own space in life.

So which one is it?

This dilemma actually reminds me of two different ideas. One is the Jewish prayer-meditation called the Havdala, which literally means the "Separation Prayer", which takes place as we end the Sabbath and go into the week.   It also reminds me of a discussion from one of my favorite books, a book by the author Stephen Covey, called The Seven Habits of Highly Effective People.

So let's break it down...

On the surface, the Havdala prayer is talking about separation. We're separating the Sabbath from the week. Or so it would seem.

After all the blessing says: "Blessed are You, God, who separates the Holy from the mundane, light from darkness, Israel from the nations, Shabbat from the six days of the week." That's how we read it quickly. And that is how almost every English prayer-book translates it.

But in Hebrew it actually says:

המבדיל בין קודש **לַ**חול

*"Hamavdil bein Kodesh **L**'chol."*

The Lamed (an 'L'-sound) at the beginning of **L**'chol in Hebrew means "toward", not "away from"!

If I was talking about a separation in the typical sense I would say "separate the Holy *away from* the mundane," which in Hebrew would be:

המבדיל בין קודש <u>מ</u>חול

'Hamavdil bein kodesh **M**'chol', with a Hebrew letter Mem.

But it says "kodesh **L**'chol," separating the Holy *towards* the mundane!

So what is the idea that the Havdala Meditation is teaching us, at the conclusion of our Shabbat of Spiritual reconnection?

First, it is saying "kodesh **L**'chol": You have spent 24 hours tapping into that which is Holy and peaceful in the world; now take that Holiness and Light, and go use it to illuminate that which you think is mundane! Because really, *everything is Holy.*

Then it says, "Ohr **L**'Choshech" — "Light toward the darkness."

Again: You separated yourself from the world for the past 25 hours in order to rediscover the Light, reconnect with how to illuminate, and find that power of illumination within you. Now it is time to cast that Light toward the places where you perceive darkness in the world! Because we all know that darkness isn't real, but merely *an absence of Light*. I can't turn off the dark. I can only turn on more Light! So darkness is merely an absence of Light. It is simply an illusion created in the spaces *where I have not yet shined my Light*, and where Light hasn't yet reached.

The Havdala continues: "Yisrael **L**'amim" — "The Nation of Israel toward all the other nations of the world."

We spoke about this last week. The idea of chosenness is not the idea of actually isolating one person from another, but rather is about setting an example that other people can follow! The gift of the Wisdom of the Torah is the gift of living in harmony, and that when a person discovers their song, when they achieve harmony, then things work out well. When they align with the Divine Flow of Life, then things work out beautifully. And when that happens, other people look and say: "Hey, why does that work for you and not for me?"

And the answer is: "Well, because I'm in a state of alignment."
"Well, why don't I have that?"
"You could."
"So what's my song? What's my message?"
"Ah. You need to find it…"

So it's *chosen in order to share* — to raise a banner that encourages everyone in the world to find *their own chosen space*, if you will. Their own unique space.

Because that's the idea: We all have a unique role to play in the world! So Yisrael **L**'amim. This is reinforcing the idea that it's not about separating Israel from the nations of the world, but rather it's about realizing our own place as the Jewish people, in order to encourage every other person in every other nation of the world to also find and celebrate their own space!

And then finally, we say "Bein Yom ha'Shevi'i **L**'sheshet Yemei ha'Ma'aseh" — "Let's bring Shabbat forward into the six days of action ahead of us."

A central theme in Jewish prayer is that every day should be Shabbat! And this is what we're saying: By discovering how to reach the inner state of alignment of Shabbat, by taking our hands out of our creative gloves of control, and *experiencing life in the beautiful way that it naturally flows* — let's bring that alignment into the way we practice and act within the week! Let's bring that kind of alignment into the week...

So what we're seeing here in this Havdala prayer, which is what's happening in our Torah portion, is that HaShem is helping us understand a certain 'Spiritual juxtaposition' if you will — a Yin-Yang of two complimentary ideas that are necessary in order to achieve and practice Spiritual alignment in life.

In order for us to find our place within the choir, we first have to train our own voice. We can't train our voice while surrounded by the hundreds of voices of the choir. If we do that, we simply disrupt the choir, and *everyone* loses their harmony.

Ultimately, at the same time, we're not looking for everyone to play the same instrument or for everyone to sing in the same key. Divine living is about harmony. It is about the coming together of each person with their unique voice, all singing together, and ultimately creating something which is spellbinding in its beauty. Divine harmony in our world occurs when we hear so many different voices singing together and complementing each other, in this shared, awesome song. It's the symphony that is played with so many different instruments coming together, creating such a powerful fusion of sound and emotion.

On the one hand God is saying: Isolate the holiness because only in the isolation do we come to appreciate the Power, the uniqueness of the Individual Element, and to hear that Voice for its Singular Power, for its Singular Force, in its Perfect Distillation. But ultimately, what that discovery and revelation is meant to do is to kindle a Spark of HaShem within each of us individually, and to inspire us to bring our Personal Sparks of HaShem out into the world in a greater conversation with the people and life that surround us.

———————————

In his book 'The Seven Habits of Highly Effective People', Stephen Covey shares a powerful idea about the three stages of human development. He talks about 'Dependence', 'Independence' and then finally, 'Interdependence'.

Dependence, he says, is the child. It's the idea that *"I can't without you.* I don't have the innate ability. I need you in order to..."

Then comes Independence, and Independence says: "I can do it on my own! I don't *need* anyone else! I have something of *my own* to offer." It's breaking free of any sense of dependency to show and to find my individual song. This emotional stage is often associated with adolescence. And in the recent changes in human culture since the 1950's, it has manifest in something we recently called the "Me Generation". It was the idea of "Me" on a social level. It's not about, so to speak, the *company man* any more. It's not about *blind patriotism*. It's the idea that I have a right to think about myself *for myself,* and to realize The Self.

But Covey then teaches us that the highest level of human performance is the level of Interdependence. Interdependence occurs once I have realized my own individual potential, and I then recognize that I am so much more effective when I work *cooperatively and in conjunction with the complementary strengths of other people*. When we come together on *that level,* we manifest a great power, because *we multiply our own unique gifts* through this cooperative, interdependent relationship with those around us. We achieve, as a community, a heightened state of social alignment.

It's interesting that Stephen Covey points out that a person cannot practice Interdependence until they truly achieve a secure sense of Independence. This is because Interdependence without a solid foundation of Independence *feels too much like dependency*. Rather than feeling this exhilaration that manifests from the cooperative harmony between people, a person without a strong foundation of Independence will feel like he or she is still needing other people in order to get done the things that he or she wants to do. And the insecurity of not having realized one's own independent strength will ultimately take on a destructive force within the greater interdependent community.

That's such a powerful idea.

And it brings me back to the two ideas we are seeing in this week's Torah portion.

In order to achieve cooperative human harmony — in order to reach that level where we literally sing together, each one playing their own instrument and each one singing their own note, forming communities of aligment within a more cooperative society — in order to reach that place, we first have to hear our own individual songs.

We first need to have that private conversation with God in the Holy of Holies, in the inner sanctuary, talking with God on this one-on-one level. We need to really isolate and recognize the Holiness, distill the Spiritual, hear the single note, hear that inner-voice calling to us in a perfectly distilled manner.

When we find that, when we can hear our Independent Voice, when we hear our Independent Calling, when we reach our Independent Song, then it's about bringing it out! Then it's about the idea of *"Make for Me a Holy Place and I will dwell in each and every one of you."*

So how do we reach that secret, Inner-Sanctuary? How do we find our Inner-Voice, our Secret Instrument?

In Chassidut, we are taught this idea of *'Hitbodedut'* — taking time every day to talk one-on-one, privately with HaShem. Not prayer. Rather, quiet reflection and very, very personal conversation with God. In your own words. From the heart. Without editing yourself at all. Straight shooting.

It is an idea of meditation that is something we see on a prevalent level among many faiths and spiritualities. And it is *SO important!*

Not just once a week. Certainly not just once a year, or only in times of personal self-interest.

It's about taking some time *each and every morning* — even if only for five or ten minutes — in order to hear your own voice, where it's just you and HaShem.

It's just you and the Source. It's just you and the Oneness of everything around you.

It should be a private time, and in a private place where no-one else can hear you speaking or see you. And you should speak to HaShem in your own words about the things that are most on your mind.

Every morning.

And I promise you, that if you do this every day for a month, you will feel HaShem answering you, too. You will feel HaShem 'dwelling within you'.

Take this time — STEAL THIS TIME!! — as much time as you need — to hear that voice, to hear your own song, to *experience* the idea of 'v'Shachanti be'Tocham, "I will dwell within you." To feel that God-Spark illuminated within you.

Consider practicing that same five minutes of quiet alignment at the end of the day, in order to realign the day you just had, as you close the day and go to sleep at night.

When you can really feel it, when you have that sense of alignment and joy, then, to open your eyes, to step outside into the world and bring that song into your day.

Taking that time of quiet reflection and personal conversation with the Divine, ultimately informs our whole day.

We enter the Holy of Holies.
We hear our personal, Singular Voice, the Distilled Voice.
And then we emerge into the public space, and bring our song — *our unique song* — into the harmony of everyone else who we will sing with throughout the day.

Week 20: The Torah Portion of 'Tetzaveh'

Raising Banners & Listening to Hearts

In this week's Torah portion, Tetzaveh, we have the making of the holy vestments, the sacred vestments that Aharon (Aaron) the High Priest is going to be wearing in the Temple. And there's one vestment called the 'Apron', which was an overgarment that Aharon wore over his tunic. The Apron had two Shoulder-Plates, and from these Shoulder-Plates hung this special device called the Hoshen Mishpat, a Breastplate which had on it the Urim v'Tumim. This was essentially a breastplate with special stones, precious stones, each one representing various Tribes.

Fascinatingly, the Breastplate & Urim v'Tumim actually served as an Oracle. When there were disputes that could not be resolved by Moshe (Moses) and by the scholars and the leaders of the Tribes, then they would go to Aharon the High Priest and the stones on the breastplate would light up, and the Urim v'Tumim — these two 'Yes-or-No' stones, if you will — would actually illuminate in order to indicate who in the argument was correct and who was incorrect. And through these light-up stones they would Divinely resolve questions that they couldn't answer purely through intellectual analysis.

This amazing device, the Breastplate and Urim v'Tumim, and the preparations for dressing Aharon, raise some interesting and meaningful questions.

Firstly, why was Aharon the one to wear this device? It is strange that Aharon should wear this device, since we know from an earlier Torah portion, Yitro, that in fact it was Moshe who was the High Arbiter of disputes among the Children of Israel.

Yitro teaches Moshe that he shouldn't be sitting in judgement alone but rather that he should set up a court system — this whole triage system — for simpler questions to be handled by 'lower courts'. More difficult questions would then be escalated to judges of greater scholarship, and ultimately only the hardest questions were to be brought before Moshe.

So Moshe is the High Arbiter of the toughest questions, and ultimately he's the figurehead of this decision making, judicial process.

So shouldn't he be wearing this Oracle, this breastplate, the Hoshen Mishpat, since ultimately this really is his role? Why is Aharon wearing this final decision-making device? Why are people being directed to Aharon when they face dilemmas that they are unable to resolve on an intellectual level?

The next question actually arises in the language the Torah uses regarding the wearing of the Hoshen Misphat, as the Torah says:

וְנָשָׂא אַהֲרֹן אֶת־שְׁמוֹת בְּנֵי־יִשְׂרָאֵל בְּחֹשֶׁן הַמִּשְׁפָּט

"Aharon should go with the names of the Children of Israel on this Hoshen Mishpat, on this Breastplate of Justice…"

עַל־לִבּוֹ

"…on his heart…"

בְּבֹאוֹ אֶל־הַקֹּדֶשׁ לְזִכָּרֹן לִפְנֵי־ה' תָּמִיד

"…when he enters into the Holy Sanctuary, as a remembrance before God always." (Exodus 28:29)

HaShem instructs that Aharon should be wearing, or 'carrying' the names of the Children of Israel, that are inscribed upon this breastplate, *upon his heart,* as a reminder before God always.

Now, if this was just supposed to be a symbol to remind Aharon of his responsibility to serve the Children of Israel, he actually already has a very effective reminder built into the Apron. Remember those Shoulder Plates? Well, it said earlier that he had the names of the Children of Israel inscribed on the shoulder plates of the apron, and it said that he should be "*traveling with them on his shoulders always.*"

He already has a reminder of his responsibilities, a very beautiful one, in that he's wearing the names of the Twelve Tribes of Israel inscribed on stones on his shoulders. So what additional message was being conveyed by his having to wear this inscribed Oracle of Truth specifically *on his heart* as a reminder?

These two questions ultimately represent two key principles of leadership that are essential to the roles we play: Whether as a parent, or as a member within a family, as a member within a social community, or as a person who might be assuming a leadership role in the immediate world or in the world at large, or even as someone who aspires toward these types of roles. And the two principles are as follows…

The first relates to why Aharon was chosen to wear this Oracle of Right and Wrong.

We live in a world today where we shy away from absolutes — absolute good or absolute evil — or that there can be any absolutes in Spiritual ideas. And we shy away from it for a very good reason. And that is because there's a lot of ugliness in the world today that stems from people claiming that they have *the patent* on Spirituality or they have the *patent* on Godliness or they have the Right Path — to the exclusion of all other Paths.

So when we see this kind of fighting and we see this kind of violence in the name of God, in the name of religion, we say, "Let's get away from these absolutes."

But while we can understand the basis of our shyness about absolutes, at the foundations of life *there really are absolutes*. Our failure to recognize and highlight them actually destroys our world, and makes it impossible for us to create a better world for ourselves and for our children, and for the future.

Stephen Covey, in the Seven Habits of Highly Effective People, discusses the idea of "Natural Laws": Natural Laws, he explains, are Truths that are self-evident to any thinking, caring, sensitive human being.   So what would some of those Natural Laws include?
- The sanctity of life.
- Fidelity in marriage.
- The nobility of giving charity.
- Helping someone in distress.

These are values, these are Principles, regarding which it is absolutely clear to us that they are inherently good things to live by.

By the same token, there are things in life that are *inherently evil*, like the wholesale murder of a human life, or to disrespect the sanctity of another person's marriage (adultery), or to lie or to be deceitful. (And we're not talking about surprise birthday parties, to be clear.)   There are certain things which are inherently destructive and which destroy the nobleness and the goodness of any society, making it impossible for a good society to flourish.

So while it is true, that on one had it is dangerous and harmful for people to run around claiming Absolute Exclusivity in an overarching relationship with God and an overarching sense of *"I know the right way to be good"*, it is equally dangerous and harmful to society if we fail to call out Genuine Truth where it is found. There *are* pillars of justice and of goodness that we *must* highlight in the world. And by the same token, there are also manifestations of evil that we have to call out and identify and seek to eliminate from our societies.

It is this Beacon of Higher Truth that Aharon represents to the Jewish people. Moshe, indeed, represents the intellectual level of seeking, erudition, and honest debate: That through discussion and scholarship and intellectual integrity, human beings have a power to distill right and wrong.

But the idea of the Hoshen Mishpat was that sometimes the dispute was not about something which should hinge upon a good argument. Sometimes we touch upon things that need to be *self-evident* on a more intrinsic level for us as human beings, based upon an imprint within our hearts and Souls that tell us what is right and what is wrong.

That's what Aharon represents. He was the High Priest. He represented that figurehead who people came to in order to bring offerings to God. He helped people connect to HaShem in their highest moments, when they were feeling great and wanted to celebrate their Spiritual connectedness, and in their lowest moments of failure and self-disappointment.

So Aharon wore the Hoshen Mishpat. Because when the discussion went beyond the intellect — when it was really about something that was not about an argument, so to speak — but rather was about illuminating the Divine Spiritual Honesty, they went to Aharon. Aharon's wearing of the Urim v'Tumim encourages each of us to raise a banner for those values which should be True and cherished by every human being.

But what about the second question regarding Aharon wearing this symbol of Intuitive Truth as a constant reminder upon his heart?

To understand the deep lesson of leadership here, we need to examine a lesson we find in the Talmud.

The Talmud tells us that if a Jewish court convicted someone to death more than once in 72 years, that court *had blood on its hands*. Wow. Heavy. Once in 72 years?? And what does that mean, that the court had blood on its hands?

The idea is this: If you have a situation in a society in which the courts are always enforcing harsh judgments upon the people, that means that the pillars of justice in that community are failing, and that the leadership is failing the community. Because the community should not have fallen into a state wherein this fierce justice must always be imposed. It is a reflection of a failure of the leadership that things should reach such a corrupted state.

Therefore, what the Talmud is teaching us is that, as much as the Torah might say that "this is punishable by stoning" and "this is punishable by lashes", the mission is **not** to punish. The mission is to raise a banner of goodness and righteousness that is so clear and so well-defined, that we never arrive at such a state of moral collapse.

This reminds me of something that a dear friend of mine, Jack Heath, shared with me. We were talking about the idea of how to help kids who are in trouble, and I shared with Jack the idea of trying to create safety nets to catch kids when they fall.

Jack replied with a very beautiful perspective. He said, "But isn't it true, Shu, that the greatest way we can help a child is by shining a light from a higher point, which distracts them or draws them away from that place of danger, and leads them to a higher place?"

To me, this idea that Jack articulated is exactly what the Talmud is teaching us, and is precisely the message of Aharon having to wear this symbol of Intuitive Truth as a constant reminder upon his heart.

What HaShem was emphasizing to Aharon was that, while Moshe might be there to arbitrate disputes, Aharon is meant to *be an example* of something that draws people to a higher place within themselves. Aharon needed to wear the Hoshen Mishpat upon his heart, because his task was to *take responsibility* for the *inner-state of moral clarity* of his community; his task was to "shine a light from a higher point that would draw his people away from the pitfalls of danger, and lead them to higher ground."

Aharon, through his sacred, wondrous services on behalf of the people in the Temple; Aharon, as a man who was known to embody the values of Peace; Aharon, as a leader wearing a Divinely illuminated Oracle with all the names of the tribes upon his heart; Aharon was there to raise a banner of True, indisputable goodness, and to declare through *his example* that there is Absolute Right and Absolute wrong in the world.

Aharon's task was to shine a light so bright, that ultimately people would aspire toward goodness. And simply as a result of doing good, there will therefore be less bad in the world. Because ultimately, the only True way to 'turn off the dark' is to turn on more and more lights — of Goodness and Truth.

This is an idea that we also see in the Garden of Eden. We're told that in the Garden of Eden, you could eat from the trees just like you could eat from the fruit. But what does that mean? It means that when you plant a tree in its native environment, the tree will grow a thinner bark than if you plant that same tree in an environment that is hostile. In a more hostile environment, that tree will grow a thicker bark. So in Eden, a tree didn't need any bark because there was nothing hostile to the tree.

What this teaches us is as follows: When we realize that principle about the tree and its bark, then what is the bark a reflection of? Is it a reflection of the tree or is it a reflection of the toxins in the environment that threaten the tree? And obviously, the latter is true.

So many times I've heard people say, "Oh, kids these days. Look at kids these days. Look at that one with his tattoo, or that one with his piercings, and that one's partying and that one's getting into this and that one's getting into that." And specifically coming from a religious community, there's always plenty of talk about how kids are turning their back on religion.

But the thing is, when a child grows a husk against their community, against their family, against the role models and the "leaders" in their lives, that's not a reflection of the child. That husk — that 'bark' you see on the tree — is a reflection of the toxins in the environment that are threatening the child.

This is a very, very important idea. It's a very deep idea. Because what it means is that, to a certain degree, the thicker and stronger the bark, arguably, the more pure and sensitive the soul behind it.

So sometimes it's that kid who everyone else is coming down on and nobody wants to talk to and everybody's condemning, who we would all benefit the most from sitting down and listening to exactly what's hurting him or her. Because he or she still possesses the innate sensitivity that can help us to understand exactly what we most need to repair in our society.

This is the meaning of telling Aharon that he should wear this breastplate — a breastplate which determines justice and determines right or wrong — on his heart all the time, as a remembrance before God at all times. Because that was the idea for Aharon to keep in mind: That ultimately the well being of the people, the decisions they're making, the right and wrong of them, reflect back upon him. If the people are shining, he's doing a great job. And if they're not, and if God forbid they're growing husks on their hearts, if they're getting into trouble, that's not a reflection of them. It's a reflection of him. It's a reflection of his leadership and Moshe's leadership, and his sons' leadership, and all those who stand before the community in a leadership role.

These two ideas are so important for us today, for each and every one of us to aspire to embody.

Firstly, there is such an urgent need in today's world to raise that banner of goodness and integrity. It's not a banner of arguments. It's not a banner of trying to prove people right or wrong. It's not an intellectual argument. But really simply raising banners of that which is intuitively good and correct, and not being afraid to shine a spotlight on that which is not good. It is about being able to call out what is good and what is bad, and what is right and what is wrong. Unapologetically. In order that we can distill our choices and ultimately get to a better place as a community, as families, and as a society.

And again, it's not about arguing. It's not about attacking.

It's about really representing.

Secondly, ultimately, is to feel these core values deeply within our individual selves, so that we all walk with that feeling in our hearts. If we stand in any kind of leadership role, even if it's just simply as a peer among our friends knowing that our decisions affect the decisions of our own closest friends, that too is a leadership role. We must realize that ultimately, when we see the husks, when we sometimes experience the negativity of those people around us, let's stop and ask ourselves: Is it them, or is it the environment they live in? Perhaps, instead of reacting to them, if I listen to them, it will help me to know where I can best put my attention, in order to make our world that much better and that much more beautiful.

May we all be blessed to raise the banner, and to feel and accept, and learn to listen, so that we can reach such a beautiful place. Together.

Week 21: The Torah Portion of 'Ki Tisah'

A Walk in the Garden of Eden

In this week's Torah portion, we find ourselves once again being instructed in the keeping of the Shabbat. This set of verses, in particular, is very meaningful. It is repeated several times during Shabbat services: First, during the Friday night service; again, in the Saturday morning service, and yet again in the Kiddush, the sanctification prayer we say before the great meal on Shabbat day.

The passage says:

וְשָׁמְרוּ בְנֵי־יִשְׂרָאֵל אֶת־הַשַּׁבָּת

"The Children of Israel will keep the Shabbat…"

לַעֲשׂוֹת אֶת־הַשַּׁבָּת לְדֹרֹתָם בְּרִית עוֹלָם

"…to practice he observance of the Shabbat throughout generations as an eternal covenant."

בֵּינִי וּבֵין בְּנֵי יִשְׂרָאֵל

"Between Me and the Children of Israel…"

אוֹת הִוא לְעֹלָם

"…it is an eternal sign…"

כִּי־שֵׁשֶׁת יָמִים עָשָׂה יְהֹוָה אֶת־הַשָּׁמַיִם וְאֶת־הָאָרֶץ

"…that in six days God created the heaven and the earth…"

בַּיּוֹם הַשְּׁבִיעִי שָׁבַת וַיִּנָּפַשׁ

"…and on the seventh day, God paused and rested."
(Exodus 31:16-17)

This poetic group of passages teaches us something beautiful. At the same time, there is something very confusing about them. Let's dive in...

Firstly, God is letting us know that Shabbat, in and of itself, is some kind of an eternal sign and covenant between God and Israel. And what is it a sign of?

It's an eternal sign that this is the world God created in six days, and then rested from active creation on the seventh day.

Most people say, "Why do we have the Shabbat? Well, we have Shabbat on the seventh day to commemorate how God rested on the seventh day. God rested, and therefore we rest."

But it says here that Shabbat is an eternal sign *that God created the world in six days, and then* rested on the seventh day.

In fact, we see in other places, like when we say the Friday-night sanctification prayer (the Kiddush), that Shabbat is actually *'zikoron l'maaseh breishit'*, that 'it's a reminder of the activities of Creation'!

How very strange, that suddenly we see Shabbat invoked as something that reminds us of the six days of Creation, that reminds us of the act of Creation! Isn't Shabbat supposed to remind us that God rested and therefore we rest? How is it that the day of rest is reminding us of the actual days of Creation?

So what is the actual meaning and symbolism of Shabbat: A symbol of Divine Rest, or a symbol of Divine Creation? And what is it about Shabbat that makes it an eternal sign, an infinite beacon of connection between us and God?

To really understand it requires us to examine what we do and what we do not do on Shabbat.

We're told that on Shabbat, we don't work. But the Hebrew word that we translate as meaning "work" is the word *malakha*. We say that on Shabbat we don't do *malakha*. It's strange that People say it means "work," because the actual interpretation of what is and is not 'melakha' suggests something quite different, and much more sublte.

You see, on Shabbat I can take my sofa, put it on my back and run around my house until I collapse. That's a lot of hard work, but it's pretty meaningless. And strangely, it does not fall into the category of forbidden 'malakha'. Yet, I am forbidden from flicking a light switch. I'm not allowed to flick a switch and turn on a light. But that's not a lot of hard work at all!

The word *malakha* actually has in its root the word *lekh*. Similarly, we have the word *Halacha,* the Hebrew word for 'Jewish Law', which also has the word *lekh* in the middle. The word *lekh* means "to go." So Halacha, the word for Jewish law, does not literally mean "law," but rather it means *HaLikha*, which I heard from my teacher Grandmaster Chaim Sober, means "The Pathway." And that's also the meaning of the word Tao. Taoism is also "The Way."

So Halacha is a Spiritual codex that provides practical guidelines by which to manifest HaLikha, The Way, The Path. It's a way of illuminating a meaningful path through life.

Similarly, *malakha*, which we translate as "work," actually is "that which derives from the way." *M* in Hebrew means "to derive from."

So on Shabbat what we refrain from doing is *malakha*. And what is *malakha*?

In the Torah, by way of the service of the Tabernacle and thereafter in the Temple, God enumerates for us 39 ways that a human being can exhibit *creative mastery over nature*. There are 39 primary forms of creative force, creative activity, that man can exert over the natural world around him or her. And these 39 practices of creative mastery are what we refrain from on Shabbat. Incredible.

Essentially, the Torah posited more than 3,500 years ago that there are 39 ways human beings show creative mastery over the natural world, and that all forms of creative activity that a human being will ever exhibit throughout the history of time forward will always be derived from, and will be able to be traceable back to, one of these 39 primary forms of creative action.

Remarkably, 3,500 years later, this is still the case. Even with all the inventions of the last century. Mind-blowing.

Let's go back to our example of the light-switch. One of the primary forms of creative activity that's delineated by the Torah is starting a fire. No argument there! We can all agree that humans starting fire is an amazing and primary act of creative power. Certainly, fire has been a tool of tremendous creative and destructive force throughout the history of humanity. Indeed, everything from guns and explosives to filament lightbulbs derive from and rely on the act of creating a spark of fire!

And so, once we recognize fire as a primary act of creative mastery, then we appreciate the wonder and power contained within the single flick of a finger on a light-switch.

With a tiny gesture, we complete a circuit that ignites a filament that's burning inside the vacuum of the lightbulb, and therefore creates a suspended flame that will burn on a fairly indefinite level. That's an amazing harnessing of the power of fire!

We know that if a little bit of air gets into a bulb, the filament instantly incinerates and we see it burn as a very bright flame for a second, and then it burns out; because the vacuum is compromised, the air rushes in, and then the filament burns very quickly and completely.

So the idea is: If fire is creative mastery over nature on a primary level, then yes, flicking a switch to complete a circuit to create this contained and sustained and suspended flame in a vacuum is an awesome act of creative power. And that's what we refrain from on Shabbat.

Now we can start to understand what the meaning is of the Sign of Shabbat.

What God tells us on Shabbat is that we, as human beings, tend to have a problem. We think the world needs us to fix it. We're always saying, "Oh, look at the world. The world is so messed up. The world needs us human beings to make it better. To fix it."

And what Shabbat says is: "Listen: Once a week, I want you to take your fingers out of your creative gloves. I want you to pull your hands out of the creative gloves that you have been given by God, that allow you to touch and manipulate the world around you. I want you to experience the world as it is, for 25 hours. Just experience it. Don't touch it. At all. Open yourself up. Become a vessel, and just feel it."

When we let go entirely — and it has to be entirely — and we open ourselves up, we suddenly realize something: That the bird knows how to sing and knows how to fly; the flower knows how to blossom; the tree knows how to grow; the wind knows how to blow.

We realize that, in fact, the world which God created in six days, and from which God then stepped back and rested on the seventh day, that perfect world is right outside our window. It's still happening. It's still just as perfect. It's still just as beautiful. And it still knows how to run perfectly and awesomely well.

Suddenly, we become sensitive to the fact that the aspects of the world that are not running so well, are the places where we, as human beings, are touching it in a destructive or harmful way.

We become sensitive to the fact that the world doesn't actually need us to fix it.

The world just needs us to live in harmony with it.
To use our creative powers wisely, and with responsibility.

This is the Sign of Shabbat.
Shabbat doesn't command us not to work.
On Shabbat, God says, "Take your fingers out of the creative gloves, the ways that you can show creative mastery over the world.

You want to run around with a couch on your back? Knock yourself out. That doesn't exert any creative force on the world around you. It will exhaust you, but it won't influence the world."

The key here is that we take our fingers out of those creative gloves, we stop touching the world on a creative level, and we experience and feel the world *as it is*.

When we do,
in that moment,
in the A-HA! of that 25-hour experience,
when we finally unplug and take ourselves out of the picture,
so that we can experience the picture in its fullness and its glory,
with an objective, still-life perspective,
we experience an Eternal Sign.

It is an Infinite Sign, because in those hours we are able to touch and to understand that the world which God created in six days, and rested within on the seventh day — it's right here with us. It's been with us all along.

It is this harmony that we take into the following week. By experiencing the alignment of Shabbat serenity, and becoming attuned to the song of the world around us, we are able then to bring our voice back into the choir of life when we let Shabbat go, and return to our six days of work.

We say the Havdalah meditation, and we bring what we have discovered forward. We bring that sanctity, that serenity, that spiritual experience forward, and return our hands to our creative gloves of power and influence. We express our own creative force, our own creative power, our own creative mastery, in a way that ultimately contributes to the song and the harmony of the beautiful world around us.

Week 22: The Torah Portion of 'Vayakhel'

Listen to the Heart

This week's Torah portion, Vayakhel, teaches us by example about one of the deepest principles of leadership, mentorship, love and friendship.

This Torah portion presents a climax, when the Children of Israel are finally bringing in the materials and engaging in the actual construction of the Mishkan, of the Tabernacle. It's important to remember the significance of the Mishkan, the first holy gathering place, or Holy Temple, for the practice of spiritual monotheism. The Tabernacle is a precursor of the Beit haMikdash, the Temple in Israel, which was the precursor of the synagogue, which was the precursor of the church and the mosque as well. And so it's a very big deal.

Before the building of the Mishkan, we had the sin of the Golden Calf. There we found the Jewish people gathering up all of their beautiful possessions and bringing them to Aaron, having him make them a magnificent cow made of gold. They then celebrated around this cow made of gold, using it as a vehicle to connect to God, or according to some interpretations, even worshipping it.

Of course, God gets very angry at the Jewish people for this. And when Moses comes down from the mountain and sees what is going on, he shatters the first set of the Ten Commandments. We all know the story...

But what is not as well known is what follows in the aftermath of that story. And that is quite a shame. Because the famous part of the story is only half-a-lesson on leadership, and half-a-lesson on parenting. It is half-a-lesson on how to address a breakdown of order — which should always come with the goal of leading those you are responsible for (which sometimes includes yourself) to a higher place.

The easy part of addressing a breakdown in order is calling out the misbehaving party for screwing up. Bosses do this quite well. So do parents. And yes, we also do this to ourselves quite a lot.

Berating others, or ourselves, for messing things up is as easy and natural as breathing. Similarly, breaking a vase — or breaking Two Stone Tablets — is pretty simple, too. It's repairing a vase that is tricky. It is carving the next set of Stone Tablets that requires artistry and patience.

And that is where real leadership is manifest. That is what transforms a typical boss into a great boss. That is what makes an average parent an amazing parent. And that is what makes our inner-voice our friend.

So let's take a look…

God tells Moshe to gather all of the Children of Israel for the building of the Mishkan. God instructs Moshe to once again invite them to participate in creating a physical, Spiritual edifice. And look at God's instructions:

וַיֹּאמֶר מֹשֶׁה אֶל־כָּל־עֲדַת בְּנֵי־יִשְׂרָאֵל לֵאמֹר זֶה הַדָּבָר אֲשֶׁר־צִוָּה ה'
לֵאמֹר: קְחוּ מֵאִתְּכֶם תְּרוּמָה לַיהוָה כֹּל נְדִיב לִבּוֹ

Moshe said to the Children of Israel, this is what HaShem has instructed: Bring gifts to HaShem, each person according to the feelings within his or her own heart. (Exodous, 35:4-5)

It's an amazing approach.

Let's try again.

From the heart.

Within a healthier framework.

The people bring gold, they bring silver, they bring colored fabrics. They bring whatever they find beautiful. In fact, for the next several pages of the Torah portion, throughout the entire chapter 35 and much of chapter 36, we see this flowing, positive manifestation of joy and alignment — all flowing from the peoples' heart.

What do they bring for the building of the Tabernacle? *Kol Nediv Lev*, whatever their heart tells them.

And who should construct the building and weave its decorations? *Kol Nediv Lev*, all those people who feel inspired in their heart to create art and architecture.

Indeed, when all the artisans and craftspeople are gathered to build the Tabernacle, the Divine instruction to the two chief artisans follows this spirit. Moshe tells the chief designers, Betzalel and Ahaliav:

אֶל כָּל־אִישׁ חֲכַם־לֵב אֲשֶׁר נָתַן יְהוָה חָכְמָה בְּלִבּוֹ כֹּל אֲשֶׁר נְשָׂאוֹ לִבּוֹ לְקָרְבָה אֶל־הַמְּלָאכָה לַעֲשֹׂת אֹתָהּ

"Include every person with an inspired heart, who feels Divine ideas stirring in his or her heart, whose heart calls him or her to be involved in this project" (Exodus 36:2)

Remarkable.

Wow.

How do we know who's an inspired artist? Anyone whose heart speaks to them.

It is such an amazing thing, this entire approach to the building of the MIshkan. God tells us: "*Show me what's in your heart*"

How will you know what to bring? "Your heart will tell you."
How will you know who should build it? "Their hearts will call to them."

Can you imagine in our modern times, an art school saying "We have a very strict criteria for who's going to be admitted into our art school: ANYONE WHO APPLIES. Yes, that's how we will know. If you apply to the art school, we will know that you are an inspired artist."

What a radical idea.

And so God introduces us to the higher form of leadership, the higher level of what to do after things go wrong. *Don't silence the heart. Yes, confront the mistake. But then, redirect the heart, honor its call, and guide it to a higher expression.*

Building on this idea of the *Inspired Heart*, the term for the Tabernacle is '*Mishkan*', coming from the Hebrew word '*Limshokh*', which means '*to draw out*'. It doesn't mean, 'to push'. Because you can't push somebody towards a spiritual experience, just like you cannot conjure love by putting a gun to someone's head. It has to be drawn out from within. It has to be discovered and drawn out from the heart.

When we built the golden calf, we offended God. Like that angry boss, or parent, or friend, or inner-voice after a screw-up, God had a right to be upset with us and to call us out.

After all, God had done so much for us, had given us so much. Ten miraculous plagues, the splitting of the sea, the revelation at Sinai. Again and again, God showered us with wonders. The pillar of fire that led us at night, the pillar of smoke that led us during the day, the Manna that was falling from heaven, all of these wonders, all of the time.

Yet we lost our way in a moment of spiritual confusion, made this massive golden statue, and started to center our worship around it, even actually saying that the statue was the god that led us out of Egypt!

So God got angry. And there was a consequence, and there was a punishment. In terms of human behavior, that part of the story — God's initial reaction — is very easy to relate to. Getting angry, dishing out a consequence for bad behavior, sending a message that "this ain't gonna fly" — that's the easy part. That's the normal reaction. That's very 'human'.

But then God goes further. He gives us this challenge, where he says, *'I want to see a better expression of what's in your heart'*. It showed the amazing, deep faith that God has in us.

A lot of times we think that the relationship with God is about *us* having to demonstrate *our* faith in *God*. But not here. Here the story is about how *God* has so much faith in *us*.

Basically, what God said is, "*Look, what you did was hurtful and upsetting. But I'm looking past the hurt now. And I'm listening to what was beneath the hurtful behavior.*"

In other words, yes, you behaved in a terrible way. But where did that behavior come from? What is at the source? Is there pain underneath that? Is there confusion underneath that? Is something missing underneath it? Where is it coming from?

True, you might not have shown your unhappiness in the right way. True, you might not have expressed your needs in the best way. But underneath that poor choice of expression, there is a need. There's something missing. There's a hunger. There's a need for validation. Whatever it is…

Loving somebody and supporting somebody is about moving past the not nice way their emotions sometimes take over. It means remembering that, while we might have to correct their behavior, we also should support them and see them, and believe in the goodness of their heart.

We don't have to be a doormat, we don't have to let people walk all over us. But when we care about someone, beyond the insult is that person's heart. Loving someone brings us a step beyond the initial anger, to ask, "*But why, why are they so upset? What's underneath? What's going on in there for real?*"

Loving them includes looking past their poor choice of expression, and showing them that we care to understand what they're really feeling inside.

HaShem saw something there, at the Golden Calf. He saw a need for a tangible way to connect to Spirituality. He saw our need for a tangible way to celebrate God in our lives. We needed some physical approach by which we could bring focus and bring context to Spiritual practice.

God's response to us was, *"I understand that. I see and believe in the good intentions inside you. I believe in your heart. Sure, building statues and bowing down around them and pointing to them as if they're Me, that ain't the way. But here, let's find a better path, together."*

"You're saying you need a way. So let's try again, with some context and guidance that I'll provide. Within that context, we will keep a space for you to express things from your heart."

"I'm not going to dictate to you what you find beautiful in your heart, or who is an artist, or what materials and fabrics you want to use. Within this healthier context — within the supporting guidance I am providing you — create your concept of beauty, and build a building that, to you, is the most beautiful thing in the world, and make it out of the materials you find most beautiful, and let it be designed by those people you find to be the best artists. And how will you know you're right? Because it's already in your heart. That's what I'm looking for."

Show me what's in your heart, and build a place — not a place of going in there and bowing down and worshiping an object. But rather, a place where people throughout history can go when they want to experience that spark of God, that point of illumination, that rests within each and every one of us.

What a lesson.

We have so much to learn from how God reacted to our poor choice of behavior. We have so much to learn from how God reacted to our emotionally misguided 'moment of ugly', our unpleasant emotional outburst, our insensitive behavior.

We face this all the time with people we love, and with people whom we can support with guidance. We face this all the time with work colleagues, with family, with friends, and with our own inner conversations with ourselves.

The question is, do we just call them (or ourselves) out, and strike out at the inappropriate behavior? Do we just shut them down?

Yes, if someone behaves in a way that's not right, you have a right, and perhaps even a responsibility, to say something. Don't be that doormat. And ultimately, not correcting the mistakes of people we care for is a disservice to them.

But after you're done addressing the insult or screw-up, take it to the next, Divine level.
Move past the mistake.
See them.
See their heart and believe in them.
And believe in yourself.

Look for the underlying, real, beautiful need that is seeking a voice.

And provide a better context for the song of the heart.

Because that song is beautiful. And we all need a safe space where we can enter, and feel the light of HaShem dwelling within each and every one of us.

Week 23: The Torah Portion of 'Pikudei'

The Axis at the Center of Our Lives

It's interesting that at the end of this week's Torah portion, Pekudei, we have the final assembling of the Holy Tabernacle, of the 'Mishkan'. There's a few notable points here.

The first, is just a strange order of events, in that the first thing we place in the Mishkan is the Holy Ark. Why is this strange?

Well, imagine the coronation of a king and queen. And imagine if the first thing we did was bring them into the empty throne-room, and then afterwards we set up the throne-room around them, and then afterwards we brought everybody in. It would seem very backwards!

Obviously, we first create the entire setting of regality and beauty and splendor, and then we have the crowning event, which is the entry of the king and queen! That's the way you'd imagine it, in terms of the whole concept of pomp and circumstance. Similarly, imagine a bride and groom: Can you imagine first having them come into an empty wedding hall, and only then setting up the wedding canopy and the entire room around them, after they're in the room?

So if you think about the idea of creating a real ceremony, we know that the Holy Ark, with the Ten Commandments inside, is really the centerpiece of the Tabernacle and the centerpiece of the Temple. But here, in terms of order, the first thing they do is they bring in the Ark with the Ten Commandments inside it. Then they bring in the Shulchan (the Ceremonial Table); they bring in the Menorah (the Holy Lamp); they bring the Incense Altar; they bring the different sacred coverings; they bring the Wash Stand. So basically, the whole rest of the Tabernacle is set up around the Ark.

It would just seem that if you want to create a meaningful ceremony, you would first set up the whole space. Then everyone would assemble, and then the final ceremony would be to carry in the Ark and place it inside, as this crowning moment of an intense "Ooh, here comes the Ark!"

So the order is strange.

There are two other things surrounding the placement of the Ark and the Ten Commandments in the Tabernacle which also really jump out.

The first is: Where were the Ten Commandments kept until now? Because basically, it says that Moses brought the Ten Commandments over to be placed into the Holy Ark:

ויקח ויתן את־העדת אל־הארן וישם את־הבדים על־הארן ויתן את־הכפרת על־הארן מלמעלה:

"Moshe took the Ten Commandments and placed them inside the ark and then they brought the ark inside the tent." (Exodus, 40:20)

The question is, where were the Ten Commandments until now?

According to at least one commentary, Nachmanides, Moses had kept them in a box in his own tent until now. Clearly, Moses had a lot of access, and a special personal relationship with the Ten Commandments. He brought them down from Mount Sinai, and he kept them with him.

Yet, all of a sudden he's going to place them in the Ark, and this Ark is going to be placed inside a sacred room within   the

Tabernacle.   And to separate this room these curtains will be hung, and this chamber will become the Holy of Holies.

From that moment forward, for the rest of time,   Moses won't have access to the Ten Commandments anymore. The only one who will have   access to the Holy of Holies is Moses' brother Aaron, the High Priest.

So there's a real change going on here. We're going from this idea of this relationship Moses had with the Ten Commandments, and the relationship he had with this component of the Jewish experience, and suddenly it's being placed entirely off limits from him. Forever.

It's changing its role from something that is connected with Moshe, into something that, from now on, only Aaron will have access to. That's a big deal! It's not just that Moses is bringing the Ten Commandments into the Mishkan, it's that he's giving up a very open role and relationship he had with them, and surrendering it to something much more restricted.

The final thing of note in this story from our Torah portion, is that after they finished setting up the entire Tabernacle, the Mishkan, it says that God's presence came to rest on it. The language here is strange:

ולא־יכל משה לבוא אל־אהל מועד כי־שכן עליו הענן, וכבוד ה' מלא את־המשכן: ובהעלות הענן מעל המשכן יסעו בני ישראל בכל מסעיהם: ואם־לא יעלה הענן ולא יסעו עד־יום העלתו:

"Moses wasn't able to enter the Mishkan because God's presence was resting in this cloud, and God's presence had filled the Mishkan. When the cloud would lift from upon the Tabernacle,

the children of Israel would travel along their journey. But if the
cloud did not lift, they would not travel until the day it would
lift." (Exodus 40:35-37)

There's a few strange things about when God's presence comes to rest upon the Tabernacle.

First it tells us that *"Moses wasn't able to enter the Mishkan because God's presence was resting in this cloud, and God's presence had filled the Mishkan."* So again we get a sense of this real change.

After all, this is the same Moses who went up Mount Sinai, where everyone saw this cloud and this presence of God resting on the mountain, and *only Moses was allowed to ascend within the cloud!* Now, all of a sudden when a cloud of Divine presence descends upon the Mishkan, *Moshe is forbidden from entering the Divine Cloud*. Something has changed.

The passage continues:

"When the cloud would lift, the children of Israel would travel, but when it didn't lift, they would not travel until the day it would lift."

This passage is very repetitive, stating the same idea twice, and we know the Torah is never superfluous with its words.

So we are faced with a strange repetition. We already know they wouldn't travel unless the Divine Cloud lifted. Yet the passage goes on to say that "when it didn't lift, *they would not travel until the day it would lift.."* When we read this repetition, describing to us in multiple ways how the Children of Israel waited, it seems to suggest *patience.* They didn't only stay put because they were commanded to do so; they were at peace with the waiting process.

We already know they didn't travel, that they only traveled when the cloud lifted. But here it emphasizes their 'waiting' from multiple angles -- not only did they travel when it lifted, but they also stayed where they were when the cloud was resting. There is a focus on both the Divine Cloud lifting and the Divine Cloud resting. It seems to be emphasizing that they were not simply waiting for a sign to make moves, but rather that they were deeply connected to the sign to be still.

There was a genuine stillness and patience being practiced here. They accepted, so to speak, the natural order of things. They allowed things to indicate the time of action and the time of inaction without pushing for one or the other.

What does all this mean?
How does it all come together?

The interesting thing is that I was struggling over these three questions, and I hadn't come up with an answer, and here it was Thursday morning, and I've got to get this ShuShine out. I was driving my daughter Revital -Shachar to school. And at this time Revi is 13-going-on-14, and a very deep thinker in her own right. So I said to her "Revi, I've got these questions for the weekly ShuShine and I'm not really sure how to answer them."

I shared with her these three questions:

- About the order of assembling the Tabernacle and bringing in the Ark and the Tablets first, and then assembling everything around them;

- The question about Moses' transitioning from having open access to the Divine, to suddenly having restricted access;

- And then seeing the way that everyone is traveling based upon the movements of the Divine Cloud, and they're patiently waiting for the changing signs in a non-pushy way.

Revi thought for a moment, and said: *"If they set up all the other furnishings of the Mishkan, and then they brought in the Holy Ark with the Ten Commandments inside them after everything had been set up, it would give you the idea that 'here's life, here's our world, and let's find a way to bring Torah, our values into it'. First set up your life, and then see if you can squeeze God and Spirituality into it."*

Revi continued, *"By first bringing in the Ten Commandments and the Holy Ark and setting them down, and then building everything around it, the message tells us: 'Here's our life, here's our values, here's what we're about. Let's build our lives around our Spiritual core.'"*

I really loved Revi's interpretation, so I went on to ask her about the issue of Moses and Aaron, and the changes in roles and access. Revi said, *"Well it seems to me that the Torah is really highlighting that at different stages in life, different people play different roles. Moshe and Aaron have different roles and missions in life, and now is the time for a change."*

Beautiful.

When I put these two ideas from Revi together with our third question, something very deep came into focus...

Many years ago, more than a decade prior, I was invited to spend Shabbat in a community in New Jersey, and asked to lead a Friday night Oneg Shabbat (for those who aren't familiar, it's when people from the community come together in someone's home, and we sit around the Shabbat table and sing songs and share spiritual insights).

So I was asked to lead one of these Spiritual get-togethers. Many parents attended, particularly because they knew about the grass-roots work I was doing at the time with hundreds of Jewish teens, and the parents wanted to hear what insights I might have to share with them.

At one point, I started to speak about how important it is to convey to our children that our Torah and its values are the number one priority in our lives.

One of the parents looked at me, and said, *"You know Rabbi? That might be true for you, because you are a Rabbi and that's how you've chosen to live your life. But not all of us are interested in being Rabbis or raising our kids as Rabbis. So that idea of the Torah being the number one priority of life, that doesn't resonate for all of us here."* A number of parents nodded their heads in agreement.

I was really shocked, and I looked at him for a minute, thinking. Finally, I asked him, *"OK, well if Torah isn't number one in your life, or in the way you want to raise your children, what is the number one, number two, or number three thing that you would have your children trade in their Torah for? What are the one or two or three things that you would have them trade for, in place of their Judaism?"*

Suddenly he and everyone at the table were very silent.

I continued, *"I didn't say your children shouldn't have careers, that they shouldn't go out and lead a lifestyle that's modern, contemporary, and very much in the same style that you have chosen to live. All I said is that the number one priority, the center of our lives, is Torah. And if it's not number one, then by definition we are suggesting that there are certain things we would agree to trade it in for, or that we compromise it for."*

This is the lesson our Torah portion is presenting us with. True to Revital's insight, this is the message of why the Ark was brought in before everything else was brought in. The message here is the idea of being really clear about what we put in the center of our lives.

Indeed, setting up the Mishkan was a lot like the idea of building a home.

When you start out as a young couple and it's just you and the person you love, you're just married, and you live in a simple apartment. Little by little, God willing, the children come and add responsibilities, along with the challenges that come with supporting a family. You find yourself going from a one bedroom or studio, to a two bedroom apartment, and then moving into a house, and taking on cars and school and tuition and all of these things.

Life grows around that first, initial commitment.

If we think of the Ten Commandments as almost like a marriage contract between God and the Jewish People, all of the other instructions and ceremonies and responsibilities and duties of our relationship with HaShem grew around that core commitment.

That's the idea, to Revital's point, of the transition from Moses to Aaron.

Moses represented someone who brings down revelation, the falling in love. There's a passage in the book of Jeremiah. God says:

זכרתי לך חסד נעוריך אהבת כלולתיך לכתך אחרי במדבר בארץ לא זרועה

"I remember your devotion to me in your youth, how you loved Me like a new bride — How you followed Me in the wilderness, in a land not yet established." Jeremiah 2:2

Moses represents revelation, the falling in love, the spark, the ah-ha! Aaron represents the service, the day to day, the ins-and-outs, ups-and-downs. That's the transition that is going on here.

When we make commitments, we decide to make something the center of life, it goes beyond the romance. When people are dating, or even when people live together, they can come and go as they please. They can say *"you know what sweetie, I'm going off backpacking with my buddies for the next three weeks. I'll try to call you as much as I can."*

But let any married man or woman try that on their spouse and it's just not going to fly! There's a responsibility in moving past casualness, in moving into an accountability, a structure, a discipline that comes when we commit to placing something in the center of our lives.

When it's the center, we build ourselves around it.
Everything else gives and takes around that which is at the center.
We don't compromise the center for those things around it.
The center can yield at times, but ultimately the center remains the center.

This message, of a higher level of commitment, of a setting of new boundaries when a commitment in our lives becomes elevated — this is what is symbolized when all of a sudden Moses sees the Cloud *and he doesn't go in*, when before he could. When casual romance, when lighthearted chilling, transitions into something real, something serious, into a central commitment of our lives and our guiding values, a structure must be put in place. Boundaries must be created. A framework of day-to-day respect, accommodation, service, responsibility, and practical devotion is essential.

Structure, healthy boundaries, and routine — as mundane as they may sound — are the pillars that turn a casual high into a sustainable high. They are the pillars that separate between casual friends and best friends. And they are the pillars of love that lasts a lifetime.

When the cloud rests, and we see the Children of Israel entering a state of patient respect until it rises again, we get a flavor, and example, of what we are challenged to bring to our relationships; with friends, with ourselves, and yes, including our relationship with HaShem. We witness a respect, a reverence, an inner-calm that embodies their commitment and devotion to that which they have placed in the center of their lives.

I want to bless each and every one of us to know what is in the center of our lives. To be able to discern those ideas, values, and principles, which truly define us, and to be able to place them with clarity in the center of our lives. May we be blessed to make decisions with responsibility and discipline and accountability, always honoring the high place of those values in the lives we lead.

About the Author

Rabbi Shu wears many hats in his life.

He is a serial startup entrepreneur, with 4 IPOs and an exit to IBM in his startup adventures.

He is an advisor to hundreds of startups, having guided them in capital raises totaling over $400 million dollars.

He is a social revolutionary, who has led multiple impact ventures that have inspired the lives of thousands of young Jews around the world to reconnect with their Jewish tradition and their inner light.

He is a rock singer and songwriter, with a published album and past performances in major venues in New York City and Tel Aviv.

He is a proud husband and father (and son and brother).

He is blessed to know God as a King, a Father, and also as a Lifelong Friend.

As a Rabbi and Spiritual Guide, Shu's 'congregation' is made up of a network of friends both young and old that span the globe, whose lives he has been fortunate to touch, and who have touched his life in return.

Shu embraces life as a Spiritual Learning-Journey, wherein all aspects of life are part of our conversation with the Divine, whether at work, at play, studying holy texts, spending time with family, chilling with friends, or dancing at a Phish show.

He deeply believes that encounters of the Soul with the Divine should be inherently loving and positive. Shu has devoted his life to illuminating this Truth by decoding day-to-day life, and connecting it with inspiring perspectives from ancient Holy texts.

Rabbi Shu lives in a farming village in the northern Negev of Israel.

You can learn more about his adventures by Googling his name, visiting his LinkedIn page, or stopping by his home for a beer and a hug.